Romantic
composers

Romantic
composers

A guide to the lives and works of the great
composers from the Romantic era

WENDY THOMPSON

southwater

This edition is published by Southwater

Southwater is an imprint of Anness Publishing Ltd

Hermes House, 88–89 Blackfriars Road, London SE1 8HA

tel. 020 7401 2077; fax 020 7633 9499

www.southwaterbooks.com; info@anness.com

© Anness Publishing Ltd 2003

This edition distributed in the UK by
The Manning Partnership Ltd,
6 The Old Dairy, Melcombe Road,
Bath BA2 3LR; tel. 01225 478 444;
fax 01225 478 440; sales@manning-
partnership.co.uk

This edition distributed in the USA and
Canada by National Book Network,
4720 Boston Way, Lanham, MD 20706;
tel. 301 459 3366; fax 301 459 1705;
www.nbnbooks.com

This edition distributed in Australia by
Pan Macmillan Australia, Level 18, St
Martins Tower, 31 Market St, Sydney, NSW
2000; tel. 1300 135 113; fax 1300 135 103;
customer.service@macmillan.com.au

This edition distributed in New Zealand by
The Five Mile Press (NZ) Ltd,
PO Box 33–1071 Takapuna,
Unit 11/101–111 Diana Drive, Glenfield,
Auckland 10; tel. (09) 444 4144; fax (09)
444 4518; fivemilenz@clear.net.nz

A CIP catalogue record for this book is available from the British Library.

Publisher: Joanna Lorenz
Managing Editor: Judith Simons
Project Editor: Felicity Forster
Editor: Beverley Jollands

Designer: Michael Morey
Jacket Design: Balley Design Associates
Picture Researcher: Cathy Stastny
Production Controller: Claire Rae

Previously published as part of a larger compendium, The Great Composers

Jacket Picture Credits: Art Archive (L'orchestre de l'Opéra by Edgar Degas);
Bridgeman Art Library (Schumann); Lebrecht Collection, London (Tchaikovsky, Wagner).

1 3 5 7 9 10 8 6 4 2

HALF TITLE PAGE: Frédéric Chopin
playing the piano in Prince
Radziwill's salon in Paris.
FRONTISPIECE: A late 19th-century
court ball at the Hofburg Palace
in Vienna.

TITLE PAGE: The French composer
Hector Berlioz, an archetypal
"Romantic" artist.

Contents

Introduction

Music is the universal language of mankind.

Henry Wadsworth Longfellow (1807–82), "Outre-Mer"

Romanticism came about in the mid 19th century as a direct reaction against the Classicism of earlier eras. Where music had previously been dominated by strict forms and structures, Romantic music was associated with literature and painting, and composers' emotional responses to nature.

This book focuses on the lives and works of the Romantic composers: those who were inspired by the poetry and drama of the great literary figures of their time, those who wrote virtuosic music for the new breed of "star" performers, the nationalistic composers who introduced native folk music into their compositions, and the later Romantics who expanded the orchestra to new dimensions and wrote music on the grand scale.

The first section of the book consists of a general history of composition from the beginnings of written musical notation up until the late Romantic era, and this is followed by the main section, which is divided into three chapters covering the great Romantic and nationalistic composers.

ABOVE: Robert Schumann (1810–56) exemplified musical Romanticism: he had a moody nature fluctuating between exuberance and depression, he maintained a prolonged struggle to win the hand of his adored Clara Wieck, and he wrote music that was highly influenced by literature.

History of composition

Beginning with the earliest forms of notation in the 9th century AD, the first section of the book traces how methods of composition have changed over time – from modes, keys, harmonization, Baroque and Classical forms to the free and emotional compositions of the Romantic composers.

The musical forms used by the principal people involved in this transformation are highlighted along the way, for example Guido d'Arezzo's "solmization" system, Pythagoras's modes, Léonin and Pérotin's *ars antiqua* and *ars nova*, Handel's *opera seria*, Bach's Baroque suites, Haydn's four-movement form and string quartets, Berlioz's programme music, Dvořák's nationalistic repertoire, Brahms's and Mahler's grand symphonies and Wagner's massive "music-dramas".

The book then charts the lives and times of the great Romantic composers, chronologically divided into the eras during which they lived.

ABOVE: The violin was used as a flamboyant solo instrument in the Romantic era, never more masterfully than by Niccolò Paganini. Paganini was a brilliant violinist, and he composed virtuosic violin music that only the most skilled could play.

The Romantic era

A central feature of much Romantic music was the portrayal of emotion. Hector Berlioz, Felix Mendelssohn and Robert Schumann, for example, wrote music that evoked dreams, visits to the countryside, and stories from literature.

Another Romantic hallmark was the composition of music for virtuosic performers. The pianist and composer Franz Liszt, for example, wrote many challenging piano works.

ABOVE: *The piano was used as a highly virtuosic instrument by many Romantic composers, and compositions were often written for specific "stars". Robert Schumann (1810–56), for example, wrote many piano pieces for his famous concert pianist wife Clara Schumann, and Franz Liszt (1811–86) performed his own innovative and technically difficult piano works.*

ABOVE: *Pyotr Ilyich Tchaikovsky (1840–93) wrote music that reflected the extremes of his temperament — moody and melancholy, but also with an intense optimism.*

The rise of nationalism

Towards the middle of the 19th century composers began to become aware of cultural differences between nations, and the nationalist movement was born. The movement spread across central Europe and was particularly strong in Russia, in the music of Nikolay Rimsky-Korsakov and Pyotr Ilyich Tchaikovsky, for example.

The later Romantics

Music in the second half of the 19th century was dominated by two rival German composers, Johannes Brahms and Richard Wagner. Brahms expanded Beethoven's principles of motivic construction, primarily writing instrumental music, while Wagner wrote operas that drew on literature, myth, drama, poetry, painting, politics and philosophy. Their combined influence was huge, for example on composers such as Giuseppe Verdi, Gustav Mahler, Jean Sibelius and Richard Strauss.

ABOVE: *Richard Wagner (1813–83) was receptive to a wide range of literary influences, and his works were almost entirely operatic. One of his aims was to unite music, drama, poetry and the visual arts, and he attempted to achieve this with his gigantic operas, the* Ring *cycle (which contains over 12 hours of music),* Tristan und Isolde, Parsifal *and* Die Meistersinger von Nürnberg. *His influence was vast and inescapable.*

History
of
Composition

A beautiful example of a medieval choirbook emanating from Germany, now in the State Library in Gdańsk, Poland. The pages illustrated show the beginning of the plainsong chant for the antiphon Rorate coeli, *used in the liturgy for the Ascension season.*

Music as a Language

We — are we not formed, as notes of music are,
For one another, though dissimilar?

PERCY BYSSHE SHELLEY (1792–1822), "EPIPSYCHIDION"

Musical composition is one of the most mysterious of all art forms. People who can easily come to terms with a work of literature or a painting are still often baffled by the process by which a piece of music – appearing in material form as notation – must then be translated back into sound through the medium of a third party – the performer. Unlike a painting, a musical composition cannot be owned (except by its creator); and although a score may be published, like a book, it may remain incomprehensible to the general public until it is performed. Although a piece may be played thousands of times, each repetition is entirely individual, and interpretations by different players may vary widely.

ABOVE: An early example of neumatic notation, from a German illustrated liturgical manuscript.

Origins of musical notation

The earliest musical compositions were circumscribed by the range of the human voice. People from all cultures have always sung, or used primitive instruments to make sounds. Notation, or the writing down of music, developed to enable performers to remember what they had improvised, to preserve what they had created, and to facilitate interaction between more than one performer. Musical notation, like language, has ancient origins, dating back to the Middle East in the third millennium BC. The ancient Greeks appear to have been the first to try to represent variations of musical pitch through the medium of the alphabet, and successive civilizations all over the world attempted to formulate similar systems of recognizable musical notation.

Neumatic notation

The earliest surviving Western European notational system was called "neumatic notation" – a system of symbols which attempted to portray the rise and fall of a melodic line. These date back to the 9th century AD, and were associated with the performance of sacred music – particularly plainsong – in monastic institutions. Several early manuscript

ABOVE: An early example of musical notation, a 3rd-century BC Greek song. The letters above the text indicate the notes.

ABOVE: *Guido d'Arezzo (c.977–1050), who devised the hexachord. His statue stands outside the Uffizi Gallery in Florence.*

sources contain sacred texts with accompanying notation, although there was no standard system. The first appearance of staff notation, in which pitch was indicated by noteheads on or between lines with a symbol called a clef at the beginning to fix the pitch of one note, was in the 9th-century French treatise *Musica enchiriadis*. At the same time, music for instruments (particularly organ and lute) was beginning to be written down in diagrammatic form known as tablature, which indicated the positions of the player's fingers.

Guido d'Arezzo

The 11th-century Italian monk Guido d'Arezzo invented the "solmization" system – the precursor of "tonic solfa" – in which various syllables were used to indicate pitches in a musical scale. He also invented the "Guidonian Hand", in which the tips and joints of the five fingers

were used as an aid to remembering the various notes. At the same time, attempts were being made to indicate rhythm in performance, by varying the length and angle of the tails of the neumes, and the earliest polyphony (the simultaneous performance of more than one melodic line) was being explored.

The modal system

From around 400 BC until AD 1500, European music was built on modes. In the 4th century BC, the Greek mathematician Pythagoras worked out a scale roughly corresponding to the (modern-day) white keys of the piano, and two centuries later this scale was being used by the Greeks in seven different ways. The early Christian church adopted four so-called "authentic" modes (corresponding to white-note scales beginning on D, E, F and G), and under the 6th-century Pope Gregory, four more modes were added for the performance of plainsong.

ABOVE: *Pope Gregory (c.540–604), who gave his name to "Gregorian" plainsong melodies for liturgical use.*

ABOVE: *The so-called "Guidonian Hand", Guido d'Arezzo's device for showing the notes of the scale.*

In 1547, the Swiss monk Henricus Glareanus postulated the theory of 12 modes, giving them somewhat inauthentic Greek names:

Dorian (range D–D)
HypoDorian (range A–A)
Phrygian (range E–E)
HypoPhrygian (range B–B)
Lydian (range F–F)
HypoLydian (range C–C)
Mixolydian (range G–G)
HypoMixolydian (range D–D)
Aeolian (range A–A)
HypoAeolian (range E–E)
Ionian (range C–C)
HypoIonian (range G–G)

Of these, the Aeolian and Ionian modes later became the basis of the minor and major scales respectively, which have since underpinned Western European music. The modes finally gave way to the keys we know today with the development of harmony in the late Renaissance period.

Emergence of Composers

Lovely forms do flow
From conceit divinely framed;
Heaven is music.

<small>THOMAS CAMPION (1567–1620), "OBSERVATIONS IN THE ART OF ENGLISH POESIE"</small>

Much medieval music survives in manuscript anthologies, some copied by monks for a particular monastery, others – often exquisitely illuminated – commissioned by an aristocratic patron. The earliest surviving ones date from the 10th century. Among the most famous manuscripts are two 15th-century English sources, the Old Hall Manuscript and the Eton College Choirbook. There are also two French sources dating from around 1470, the beautiful heart-shaped *Chansonnier cordiforme* and the *Mellon chansonnier*. Many pieces in these manuscripts are anonymous, but some were attributed to individual composers.

Ars antiqua

The Parisian composers Léonin and Pérotin were among the finest exponents of the style called *ars antiqua*, or "ancient style", a method of harmonizing plainsong melodies by adding between one and three secondary voices to the main vocal line, moving in parallel motion. This was known as *conductus*, and was an early form of polyphony – a compositional technique in which several melodic lines are combined, moving independently (as opposed to

homophony, in which the voices move together, forming blocks of harmony). European music was dominated by the polyphonic principle from the 13th to the 16th centuries.

By the 13th century, musical notation had become more sophisticated and standardized, with only the finer points of rhythmic

notation still open to interpretation. *Conductus* was gradually superseded by a new form known as the motet, a sacred Latin song, usually with a Biblical text, in which other voices moved in counterpoint to the main tune. The motet has remained a standard form of liturgical music.

Ars nova

At the same time, secular songs, such as those sung by French troubadours and *trouvères*, were being written down. Their flexibility and tunefulness led to the development of a new style (*ars nova*) in the 14th century, initiated by the theorist Philippe de Vitry. The music of the *ars nova*, which flourished particularly in France and Italy, had greater rhythmic vitality, and composers such as Guillaume de Machaut began to experiment with new techniques such as isorhythm, in which the same rhythmic pattern appears in successive repetitions of the melody, but not necessarily using notes of the same value. Many motets of the period were based on this technique, and on a *cantus firmus* – a familiar tune (either a plainsong melody or a folk song) which underpinned a polyphonic composition

ABOVE: An example of the ars antiqua *– a page from the* Jeu de Robin et Marion *by Adam de la Halle (1230–c.1288).*

ABOVE: An example of ars nova notation – an anonymous 14th-century French virelai (song). Note the increasing complexity of the notation.

increasing sophistication of musical instruments. This was the invention of "monody", a new style in which the old principle of equal voices moving in counterpoint gave way to a single vocal line accompanied by instruments. While the tenor line still carried the main tune of a composition, it was now underpinned by a "ground bass", or *basso continuo* – a strong bass line played on keyboard and reinforced by cello and other bass instruments, which provided a harmonic foundation. The new style – the basis of all Baroque music – originated in Florence, where the composer Giulio Caccini published a famous collection of monodies, *Nuove musiche*, in 1602. The invention of monody coincided with the birth of a new secular musical genre, opera. The concept of a drama set to music, performed by costumed singers with instrumental accompaniment, originated in Florence with early examples by Peri and Caccini. Its greatest early exponent was Claudio Monteverdi.

ABOVE: An exquisitely illuminated page from the 15th-century Squarcialupi codex showing Francesco Landini (c.1325–97) with the score of his madrigal Musica son.

by appearing throughout, usually in the tenor line.

By 1500 the system of Western European musical notation had become largely standardized, and from then onwards it became increasingly sophisticated and refined. The 16th century (the High Renaissance) was dominated by the principle of polyphony, brought to a height of perfection by composers such as Palestrina in Italy, Lassus in Germany, Victoria in Spain, and William Byrd in England.

Radical change of style

Around 1600, a musical sea-change occurred, partly as a reaction against polyphony, partly as a result of the secularization of society, and the

Baroque Forms

Music in the Baroque era (c.1600–1750) was dominated by an insatiable demand for recreational art-forms. The great aristocratic and royal households, which could support their own orchestras, also employed composers to supply a constant need for new works. In 18th-century Europe, the growing size and wealth of the new middle classes led to a gradual democratization of musical appreciation and the advent of public performances in new concert halls and opera houses.

ABOVE: A sumptuous court entertainment of 1747 in the Teatro Argentina in Rome to celebrate the marriage of the son of Louis XV.

Music and drama

Opera became a favourite entertainment at the many princely courts which dotted Europe; the first public opera house opened in Venice in 1637, followed by others in major European cities. New musical forms were developed to suit the genre, including recitative and aria: the recitative allowed the singer (accompanied only by keyboard) to advance the story rapidly; while the aria, accompanied by the orchestra, allowed for expansive and lyrical reflection on a given situation or emotion.

The Baroque era was dominated by *opera seria*, based on plots drawn from ancient mythology, legend or history, with heroic characters fulfilling their destinies according to approved behavioural concepts. The most prolific 17th-century opera composers included Alessandro Scarlatti and Antonio Vivaldi in Italy, Reinhard Keiser in Germany, and Jean-Baptiste Lully in France.

But by far the greatest exponent of Italian *opera seria* was Handel, who managed to make his characters express real human emotions. His operas have survived, while works by his contemporaries have been consigned to history. *Opera seria* lasted into Mozart's time, but by then audiences were demanding a lighter, more naturalistic type of drama, often dealing with comic subject-matter, which flowered in the hands of Gluck and especially Mozart.

Oratorio

Despite initial resistance, not even the church could remain unaffected by these new developments. A sacred – and normally unstaged – type of musical drama called oratorio, using the same musical forms as opera, but based on biblical stories, came into being. Most opera composers (such as Scarlatti and Vivaldi) also wrote oratorios, but again it was Handel's fine examples which have survived to the present day. Bach's *St John* and *St Matthew Passions*, relating the story of Christ's death according to the Gospels, belong to this genre.

Instrumental forms

A growing demand for purely instrumental music led to the development of other new forms, such as the sonata. This was conceived both as a form suitable for church performance – the *sonata da chiesa*, which the Italian composer Corelli developed as a standard four-movement form – and its lighter counterpart the *sonata da camera*, which had an unspecified number of dance-like movements. Dance types – gavotte, minuet, courante, allemande, gigue – found their way into instrumental compositions, and their enormous variety formed the basis of the Baroque suite, perfected by Bach and Handel.

Another new form was the concerto, a genre pioneered by Giovanni Gabrieli in the late 1500s, in which a small group of instruments (later one solo instrument) is contrasted with the main body of the orchestra (the earlier form is known as a *concerto grosso*). While Renaissance music had exalted the principle of equality, Baroque music thrived on contrast.

Transition to Classicism

The still, sad music of humanity.

WILLIAM WORDSWORTH (1770–1850), "TINTERN ABBEY"

ABOVE: A group of musicians playing stringed and keyboard instruments at the court of the Duke of Modena in the late 17th century, painted by Antonio Gabbiani (1652–1726).

Baroque music reached its zenith in the works of Bach and Handel. Bach concentrated on sacred music, notably in his many cantatas – dramatic works for voices and instruments intended for church performance; Handel worked in both secular and sacred genres, writing Italian operas and English oratorios. The opening instrumental overtures, or "sinfonias", of such pieces gradually expanded into the 18th-century symphony, which eventually settled into a standard four-movement form with an opening fast movement, a lyrical slow movement, a short dance movement (usually a minuet and trio) and a fast finale. This was the form which Joseph Haydn perfected in over 100 examples, together with another new instrumental genre, the string quartet, written for two violins, viola and cello.

Sonata form

These works, together with the Classical sonata itself, were dominated by the structural principle of "sonata form", in which an opening exposition, usually presenting two main, contrasting themes, is succeeded by a central "development" section, in which the themes are subjected to a variety of treatments. Then comes a "recapitulation", in which the opening themes are repeated (often in shortened or slightly varied form), followed by a short "coda" to round off the movement.

Haydn's great Viennese contemporaries Mozart and Beethoven consolidated and developed the symphony and string quartet, as well as the solo concerto – which was now becoming primarily a vehicle for one virtuoso performer. As the 18th-century harpsichord gave way to the more powerful and reliable pianoforte, the piano concerto – and the solo piano sonata – became favoured forms from Mozart's time onwards.

ABOVE: An 18th-century concert with wind, string and keyboard players held at a private Italian palazzo (probably in Venice).

The Romantic Heyday

There is nothing stable in the world; uproar's your only music.

JOHN KEATS (1795–1821)

While Napoleon Bonaparte swept across Europe, toppling the decadent aristocratic rulers of the *ancien régime*, Beethoven's powerful musical vision heralded a new age of individualism. His massive *Eroica* Symphony (No. 3) pushed Classical symphonic form to its limits, while his Sixth (*Pastoral*) Symphony showed how music could be used to illustrate humanity's relationship with nature (a favourite concept of the Romantic era, as illustrated in the art and literature of the period). Meanwhile, as aristocratic patronage declined, the burgeoning middle classes began to demand music on a domestic scale for private enjoyment – a market filled by the music of

ABOVE: One of the seminal literary works of Romanticism – an artist's impression of Goethe's Faust in his study, painted in 1829.

Schubert, Schumann, Chopin, Mendelssohn and Brahms, who produced songs with piano accompaniment, chamber music (for combinations of string and wind instruments) and solo piano pieces.

The rapid expansion of the orchestra during this period, together with the invention of new instruments such as the clarinet and the improvement of existing ones, particularly woodwind and brass, led to the creation of much larger ensembles with increased power, colour and tonal range. These demanded new types of music on a vastly expanded scale. In line with the expansionist vision of the 19th century, the symphonic canvases of Schumann, Brahms, Bruckner and Mahler became

ABOVE: A typical Romantic seascape: Moonrise over the Sea, *by Caspar David Friedrich (1774–1840).*

ABOVE: *An impression of Wotan from Wagner's massive operatic cycle* Der Ring des Nibelungen *(1853–74).*

ABOVE: *The Russian composer Nikolay Rimsky-Korsakov was the most prominent member of "The Mighty Handful". His nationalistic works include* Voskresenaya *(Russian Easter Festival Overture) and the opera* Sadko, *a setting of Russian folk legends.*

ever more inflated; while Wagner's massive "music-dramas", culminating in the epic saga *Der Ring des Nibelungen*, first performed complete in 1876, pointed the way forward to the "music of the future".

Rise of nationalism

While Germany led the musical world in symphonic terms, composers such as Smetana and Dvořák in Bohemia, Glinka, Borodin and Rimsky-Korsakov in Russia, Grieg in Norway and Chopin in Poland were beginning to discover an individual musical culture by introducing the colourful inflections of their native folk music into standard musical genres. Liszt, the Hungarian composer and virtuoso pianist, tackled the symphony from a different angle, inventing the one-movement symphonic "tone-poem" (usually inspired by a poetic, artistic or literary idea); this form was later adopted by Richard Strauss.

For much of the 19th century, England languished as "the land without music" until it was rescued from oblivion on the one hand by the enchantingly witty "Savoy Operas" of Gilbert and Sullivan, and on the other by the genius of Edward Elgar, the first major British composer since Purcell. Italy, however, continued to consolidate its reputation as the operatic centre of the world, with masterpieces by Rossini, Donizetti, Bellini, Verdi and Puccini.

ABOVE: *A poster advertising three operas by Gilbert and Sullivan –* The Gondoliers, The Mikado *and* The Yeomen of the Guard *– produced by the D'Oyly Carte Opera Company.*

Romantic Composers

The Ride of the Valkyries, *inspired by an episode from Act III of* Die Walküre
by Richard Wagner, painted by William T. Maud (1865–1903).

The Romantic
❧ Era ❧

*Dancers at a court ball at the Hofburg Palace in Vienna in the late
19th century, painted by Wilhelm Gause.*

Drama and Poetry in Music

Music, moody food
Of us that trade in love.

WILLIAM SHAKESPEARE (1564–1616), "ANTONY AND CLEOPATRA"

Schubert represented a turning-point in musical history. He inherited the Classical forms of his predecessors, but while his own musical style was essentially Classical, his inspiration looked forward to the age of Romanticism. One of the key features of Romantic music is its strong association with other art-forms, particularly literature or painting. Schubert responded instinctively to the poetry and drama of the great literary figures of his time: Goethe, Friedrich Schiller, Friedrich Rückert, Friedrich Klopstock, and Ludwig Hölty. Their writings, even when dealing with historical figures or events, expressed ordinary human emotions – love, happiness, sorrow – and the beauty of the natural world. One of the most potent examples of literary Romanticism was Goethe's epistolary novel *Die Leiden des jungen Werthers* (*The Sorrows of Young Werther*), published in 1774. It was inspired by Goethe's own unrequited love for a friend's fiancée, and the news of another friend's suicide as a result of disappointed love. *Werthers* had an enormous influence on European youth, and the theme of frustrated passion became a common one in the literature of the period.

Untamed nature

The other great Romantic theme was a response to nature, especially in its wilder aspects. Earlier generations had sought to tame and cultivate the landscape; but in the late 18th century artists and writers – spurred on by Jean-Jacques Rousseau (1712–78) and his rejection of rationalism – reacted against the artificial moral code of Classical writers and philosophers, who believed in a neatly ordered world. Artists such as Théodore Géricault, J. M. W. Turner and Caspar David Friedrich began to depict the puny, helpless nature of human beings when pitted against terrifying natural phenomena such as avalanches or storms; while writers such as Lord Byron, William Wordsworth, Percy Bysshe Shelley and Sir Walter Scott identified human emotions with the turbulent moods of nature, and drew

ABOVE: This dramatic snow-capped landscape entitled Near Chamonix *was painted by James Stormont in the 19th century. Views such as this inspired many Romantic composers to write music that celebrated the beauty and ruggedness of nature.*

ABOVE: *A caricature by Gustave Doré of Berlioz conducting at the Jardin d'Hiver (Winter Garden) in Paris, 1850.*

inspiration from the rugged landscapes of northern Europe, especially Scotland, or from the remoter, brigand-infested parts of Italy and Greece.

Portrayal of emotion

This was the climate which produced the great musical masterpieces of early Romanticism. Among these are Schubert's song-cycles *Die schöne Müllerin*, in which the brook (represented in the piano accompaniment) becomes an equal partner in a drama of rejection and suicide; and *Winterreise* (*Winter Journey*), in which both singer and accompanist paint a vivid picture of wintry desolation, mirroring the bleak emptiness in the betrayed protagonist's soul.

Berlioz left no listeners in any doubt about the "programme" behind his

orchestral masterpiece, the *Symphonie fantastique*, in which a young opium addict dreams he has killed his beloved and is led to the guillotine; while Mendelssohn's orchestral music records his vivid impressions of visits to Italy and Scotland. Much of Schumann's music was inspired by literary models; like Schubert, he had an immediate and passionate response to literature. At the same time, Liszt's newly invented "tone-poem" proved an ideal vehicle for musical responses to literature or art.

Virtuoso performers

The other hallmark of musical Romanticism was its emphasis on the individual – either the composer, fighting a lonely battle against incomprehension and intolerance, or the performer. The 19th century saw the rise of the star performer, and with it a division between creator and executant which became progressively more marked in the 20th century. Many 19th-century composers

ABOVE: *A poster advertising Massenet's opera* Werther *(1887), based on Goethe's novel* The Sorrows of Young Werther.

(Chopin, Liszt, Brahms, Paganini) carried on the tradition followed by Mozart and Beethoven in writing music for themselves to perform, but they also began to write for other virtuoso executants, such as the pianists Clara Schumann (1819–96), Eugen d'Albert (1864–1932) and his wife Teresa Carreño (1853–1917); the violinists Joseph Joachim (1831–1907), dedicatee of concertos by Brahms and Bruch, Ferdinand David (1810–73), for whom Mendelssohn wrote his concerto, and Pablo de Sarasate (1844–1908), for whom Lalo, Bruch and Saint-Saëns wrote concertos; and the clarinettist Richard Mühlfeld (1856–1907), for whom Brahms wrote his great chamber works for that instrument.

ABOVE: *A painting by Edgar Degas (1876) of the divertissement in Meyerbeer's 1831 opera* Robert le diable, *seen from the viewpoint of the orchestra.*

Gioacchino Rossini

Rossini, in music, is the genius of sheer animal spirits.

LEIGH HUNT (1784–1859)

Towards the end of the 18th century, Italy was producing many composers of entertaining, accomplished, but undeniably ephemeral operas. Composers such as Giovanni Paisiello and Domenico Cimarosa wrote dozens of stage works, but very few survived for more than a season, and none could match the Italian masterpieces of Mozart. Opera in Italy had become stereotypical, subject to the tyrannical demands of audiences for a constant stream of hurriedly composed new works, and of singers for arias to show off their vocal technique, in defiance of dramatic exigencies. Italy needed an outstanding opera composer, and found one in the person of Gioacchino Rossini.

Rossini was the son of a horn player and a singer, and began to compose as a child. In 1806 he went to study at the Liceo Musicale in Bologna, and at the age of 15 was commissioned to write his first opera, *Demetrio e Polibio*. Further commissions followed, including several from the Teatro San Moïse in Venice for a series of one-act *farse* including *La scala di seta* (*The Silken Ladder*, 1811) and *Il Signor Bruschino* (1813).

Productive years

Rossini was able to work at high speed, and between 1810 and 1822 he turned out a steady flow of works, both comic and serious, for production in Venice, Milan, Naples and Rome, none of which took him more than a few weeks to write.

ABOVE:
A portrait of Gioacchino Rossini (1792– 1868), now in the Liceo Musicale in Bologna where he studied.

LEFT:
The interior of the Teatro San Carlo in Naples, where several of Rossini's operas were first performed.

Life and works

NATIONALITY: Italian

BORN: Pesaro, 1792; **DIED:** Paris, 1868

SPECIALIST GENRES: Opera (both "serious" and comic).

MAJOR WORKS: *Il barbiere di Siviglia* (1816); *La cenerentola* (1817); *Semiramide* (1823); *Guillaume Tell* (1829); Stabat Mater (1832–41); *Petite messe solennelle* (1863).

Among them were the serious operas *Tancredi*, *Elisabetta*, *Regina d'Inghilterra* and *Otello* (based on Shakespeare's play), and the comic operas *L'italiana in Algeri* (The Italian Girl in Algiers), *Il barbiere di Siviglia* (The Barber of Seville – Rossini's comic masterpiece), *La cenerentola* (Cinderella), and *La gazza ladra* (The Thieving Magpie). Of these, *The Barber of Seville* (based on Beaumarchais's prequel to *The Marriage of Figaro*) was a disappointing failure at its Roman première in 1816, thanks to a catalogue of onstage disasters, though by its third performance it had recovered from its initial setback. In one version of a famous story about Rossini, who was a notorious gourmet, he was asked by a journalist whether it was true that he had cried in public only twice in his life – the first time after the première of *The Barber*, and

ABOVE: A set for an 1830 production of Rossini's opera Le siège de Corinthe *(The Siege of Corinth) at the Berlin State Opera.*

the second when a particularly delicious piece of turkey stuffed with truffles had fallen in the river during a picnic. Rossini pondered, and then answered: "No, only once, and that was when the turkey fell in the river."

Rossini's greatest *opere serie* were written for the Teatro San Carlo in Naples between 1817 and 1823: they included *Mosè in Egitto* (Moses in Egypt), *La donna del lago* (based on Walter Scott's *The Lady of the Lake*), *Maometto II*, and *Semiramide*, the last of his Italian operas. In 1822 he married the singer Isabella Colbran, who had created the soprano roles in many of his operas, and after trips to Vienna and London, he settled in Paris as director of the Théâtre-Italien. He was still only 31 years old, rich and famous, with 34 operas to his credit.

Later life

Over the next six years he wrote several more operas for Paris, but after *Guillaume Tell* (*William Tell*), arguably his finest work, he effectively retired. In 1836 he returned to Italy, where he suffered prolonged periods of ill-health, but finally settled in Paris again with his second wife Olympe Pélissier, devoting himself to entertaining friends and eating (he invented, among other dishes, *tournedos Rossini*). The

only musical products of his later life are the delightful series of salon pieces which he called "the sins of my old age", and two sacred works, a Stabat Mater and the *Petite messe solennelle*.

Rossini's music

In the operatic field, Rossini's innovations included the replacement of keyboard-accompanied recitative by orchestral accompaniment, the expansion of the chorus and its dramatic integration, the development of the coloratura aria, and the revitalization of *opera buffa*; his characters, such as Figaro and the delightful Rosina, are real people with whom audiences of all ages can identify. His brilliant opera overtures (characterized by their famous, whipped-up *crescendo* endings) are still often performed in the concert repertoire today.

ABOVE: The title page of the fifth edition of the vocal score of Rossini's last opera, Guillaume Tell, *published in Paris.*

ABOVE: An 1829 cartoon by A. E. Chalon of the character of Figaro, the hero of Rossini's Il barbiere di Siviglia.

Carl Maria von Weber

*Weber, who seems to whisper in my ear like a familiar spirit,
inhabiting a happy sphere where he awaits to console me.*

HECTOR BERLIOZ (1803–69)

Carl Maria von Weber, a leading pioneer of the German Romantic and nationalist movement, is chiefly remembered today for his opera *Der Freischütz* (*The Free Shooter*), the sparkling piano piece *Aufforderung zum Tanz* (*Invitation to the Dance*) which was orchestrated by Berlioz, the *Konzertstück* for piano and orchestra, and his brilliant works for clarinet.

Weber was born into a musical family in northern Germany, the son of a theatrical impresario and a singer. He took music lessons as a boy with Joseph Haydn's brother Michael in Salzburg, and by the age of 14 had already written his first opera. He completed his musical education in Vienna, and then spent over a

ABOVE: A portrait of Carl Maria von Weber (1786–1826) by Caroline Bardua.

decade working at various courts and municipal theatres in Germany (during which time he wrote many of his instrumental pieces) before being appointed director at the Prague Opera in 1813. During his tenure there he fell in love with the singer Caroline Brandt, but their tempestuous courtship lasted for four years before they were married.

ABOVE: Costume designs for villains Samiel and Caspar in Der Freischütz *(1821).*

A new German opera

On Christmas Day 1816 Weber was appointed to the prestigious post of *Kapellmeister* at the Dresden court. His brief was to establish a national German opera to rival the current dominance of the Italians, and throughout his time at Dresden he had to contend with the overt hostility of the royal *Kapellmeister* (an Italian), as well as with the early symptoms of tuberculosis. Nevertheless he persevered with building up his opera company, and with the composition of his German opera *Der Freischütz*.

The première of *Der Freischütz* in Berlin on 18 June 1821 was

Life and works

NATIONALITY: German

BORN: Eutin, near Lübeck, 1786; **DIED:** London, 1826

SPECIALIST GENRES: German Romantic opera, works for clarinet.

MAJOR WORKS: Two clarinet concertos; Clarinet Quintet (1814); *Grand Duo Concertant* (1816); *Aufforderung zum Tanz* (1819); *Konzertstück* in F minor (1821); *Der Freischütz* (1821); *Euryanthe* (1823); *Oberon* (1826).

ABOVE: Berlin in Weber's time – a view of the Brandenburg Gate and the Pariser Platz.

Oberon, commissioned by the manager of the Covent Garden Theatre in London, was scheduled for performance in the spring of 1826. By the end of 1825 Weber knew that he was dying. Athough his wife and friends tried to dissuade him from travelling to London to conduct the opera, Weber was so worried about making financial provision for his young family that he insisted on making the journey.

He managed to conduct the première of *Oberon* on 12 April 1826, also undertaking many other concert engagements, but he was failing fast. He died at his lodgings in Great Portland Street in London on 5 June, aged only 39. Eighteen years later, Wagner, whose own early operas in the German Romantic style owed an enormous debt to Weber's pioneering work, had his predecessor's remains taken back to Dresden.

a triumph. Compared with the stuffy court operas of the period, it was entirely fresh and riveting, based on a story drawn from German folklore, and with music strongly influenced by German folk song idioms – the music of the people. It is based on the tale of a young forester who tries to win the hand of his beloved by selling his soul to the Devil in return for seven magic bullets which cannot fail to hit their targets. This gave Weber the opportunity for a marvellous supernatural scene in the "Wolf's Glen", a gift to designers and producers, with spine-chilling music to match.

Although *Der Freischütz* went on to take Europe by storm, Weber's next two operas were less successful. Both *Euryanthe* and *Oberon*, while containing marvellous individual numbers (the overture to *Oberon* is a masterpiece), suffered from muddled, incomprehensible plots and little sense of drama. *Euryanthe* opened in Vienna in 1823, but was given only 20 performances.

ABOVE: The "Wolf's Glen" scene from Der Freischütz *– the 1982 production of Weber's famous opera performed at the Royal Opera House in Covent Garden, London.*

Hector Berlioz

*Berlioz composes by splashing his pen over the manuscript
and leaving the issue to chance.*

FRÉDÉRIC CHOPIN (1810–49)

Like Schumann and Chopin, Berlioz is regarded as an archetypal "Romantic" artist, both for the nature of his work and for the colourful events of his life, which are documented in his entertaining *Memoirs*.

The son of a provincial French doctor, he intended to pursue a medical career, but the grisly scenes of carnage he encountered at medical school in Paris put him off. Instead he began music lessons, first privately and then at the Paris Conservatoire.

ABOVE: Hector Berlioz composing his opera Les Troyens *(The Trojans).*

Scaffold", the artist dreams that he has murdered his beloved and is being led to the guillotine; in the last, a grotesque witches' sabbath, the beloved has been transformed into a hag, her theme obscenely distorted.

In 1832 Berlioz finally persuaded Harriet Smithson to marry him. But proximity to the Beloved proved less appealing than worship from afar. Although he never divorced Harriet (who died of alcoholism in 1854), he formed a liaison from 1841 onwards with the

Sensitive, passionate and impulsive by nature, Berlioz was prone to violent emotions. In 1827 he saw an English theatre company performing *Hamlet* at the Odéon Theatre, and was immediately stricken with wild admiration, both for Shakespeare and for Harriet Smithson, the attractive Irish actress who played Ophelia. His unrequited passion found an outlet in 1830 in the extraordinary, programmatic *Symphonie fantastique*, subtitled "Episodes in the life of an artist". In the first three of its five movements, "the beloved" appears in various transformations as a melodic motif (which Berlioz called the *idée fixe*), whether in "passions and dreams", at a ball, or during a pastoral idyll (which owes much to Beethoven). In the fourth movement, "March to the

ABOVE: A cartoon of Berlioz conducting, surrounded by some of the bizarre instruments he deployed – including a cannon!

ABOVE: Harriet Smithson as Ophelia. Berlioz became obsessed with her and eventually married her, with disastrous consequences.

singer Marie Recio, who later became his second wife.

During the 1830s Berlioz produced some of his finest works, including the symphony with obbligato viola, *Harold en Italie*. This work was commissioned by Paganini, who paid the struggling composer 20,000 francs for the piece, although he never played the solo part because he said it did not adequately display his talents as a virtuoso.

Large-scale works

Berlioz's predilection for the monumental led him to compose enormous scores for huge orchestral forces (although he himself played only the guitar, he was a master of orchestration and wrote an influential treatise on the subject). His colossal works for chorus and orchestra included a Requiem (1837), the dramatic symphony *Roméo et Juliette* (1838–9), the *Grande symphonie funèbre et triomphale* (1840), and the

operas *Benvenuto Cellini* (1834–7), and *Les Troyens* (*The Trojans*, 1856–8).

Berlioz never had enough money. He was forced to supplement his income by working as a music critic, and by touring Europe as a conductor. In 1846 *La damnation de Faust*, a "dramatic cantata" based on the play by Goethe – whom Berlioz declared, together with Shakespeare, the guiding influence of his life – failed to attract attention in Paris, though it scored a great success in Russia. But his oratorio *L'enfance du Christ* (*The Childhood of Christ*) achieved a modest success in 1854, and the exquisite "Shepherds' Farewell" scene has always remained a popular favourite.

Les Troyens finally reached the stage in 1863, when the second part only, *Les Troyens à Carthage*, was performed in Paris. Its failure broke Berlioz's heart, and his last years were clouded by depression and ill-health. (The opera was not staged in its entirety in French until 1969.) In the early 1860s he completed his last work, the

sparkling Shakespearean opera *Béatrice et Bénédict*, but thereafter wrote little until his death.

Re-evaluation

While his large-scale works are still performed relatively infrequently because they are so expensive to mount, the *Symphonie fantastique* and the concert overtures (especially *Les francs-juges*, the Byronic *Le corsaire* and *Le carnaval romain*) have remained popular, as has the delicately scored orchestral song-cycle, *Les nuits d'été* (*Summer Nights*, 1841), based on a series of poems by Théophile Gautier.

Berlioz is still perceived as an "oddball" composer, and his originality has been derided as incompetence. But the persuasive advocacy of writers such as David Cairns and conductors such as Colin Davis and Roger Norrington have restored some previously neglected masterpieces, such as *Les Troyens*, to the repertoire, and affirmed Berlioz's importance as one of the foremost 19th-century composers.

ABOVE: *Caricature of Berlioz conducting, by Georges Tiret-Bognet (born 1855).*

Felix Mendelssohn

A romantic who felt at ease within the mould of classicism.

PABLO CASALS (1876–1973)

Felix Mendelssohn was born into a wealthy and cultured Jewish family. His grandfather Moses was a liberal philosopher, and his father, Abraham, a prominent banker who fled from Hamburg (where Felix and his sister Fanny were born) to Berlin, to escape Napoleon's marauding troops. The Mendelssohn family enjoyed a privileged middle-class existence in Berlin, where the children (two girls and two boys) were baptized as Christians, and their father became a town councillor.

At the family home, the young Felix encountered many well-known philosophers, actors, artists, writers and musicians, and showed precocious talent in music, drawing and poetry. By the age of 13 he was already an accomplished composer, and in 1821 he was introduced by his teacher Karl Zelter to Goethe. A strong friendship

ABOVE: *Felix Mendelssohn (1809–47), painted by Gustav Zerner.*

based on shared interests developed between the literary giant (then aged 70) and the talented boy. Mendelssohn dedicated his Third Piano Quartet to Goethe, who greatly appreciated the young man's frequent visits to his home in Weimar.

Musical impressions

Mendelssohn travelled a great deal as a young man, visiting Switzerland, Italy and Britain. He responded passionately both to literature and to impressions of people and landscapes encountered on his travels, both of which influenced his essays in the Classical musical forms of his day – symphony, overture, concerto, sonata and quartet. At the age of 16 he composed the brilliant Octet for strings, whose scherzo was inspired by the "Witches' Sabbath" scene in Goethe's *Faust*; two early overtures were inspired

LEFT: *The Leipzig Conservatory of Music, founded by Mendelssohn in 1843.*

RIGHT:

The autograph score of the first of Mendelssohn's six Songs Without Words *for piano (1829).*

Life and works

NATIONALITY: German

BORN: Hamburg, 1809;
DIED: Leipzig, 1847

SPECIALIST GENRES:
Symphonies, overtures,
concertos, piano pieces, songs.

MAJOR WORKS: Five
symphonies; incidental music
to *A Midsummer Night's Dream*
(1826–42); Octet for strings
(1825); *Hebrides* overture
(1830); Violin Concerto
(1844); two piano concertos;
eight books of *Lieder ohne Worte*
(*Songs Without Words*) for piano
(1829–45); *Elijah* (1846).

respectively by Shakespeare (*A
Midsummer Night's Dream*) and Goethe
(*Calm Sea and Prosperous Voyage*). Two
of his five mature symphonies – the
Scottish (No. 3, dedicated to Queen
Victoria) and the *Italian* (No. 4) –
reflect his impressions of landscapes.
His 1829 tour of Scotland also inspired
the famous *Hebrides* overture, written
after a visit to Fingal's Cave on the Isle
of Staffa.

Classical style

In Mendelssohn's two piano concertos,
the much-loved Violin Concerto and
the *Scottish* Symphony, he made
original experiments in form, such as
the recycling of thematic material and
the linking of movements, which later
became a feature of much Romantic
music. Yet, for all his Romantic
traits, he was a worthy successor
to Beethoven and Schubert in his
fluent handling of musical material.
Schumann called him "the Mozart of
the 19th century – the one who sees

most clearly through the contradictions
of the period and for the first time
reconciles them".

Mendelssohn's musical legacy

Through his tireless work as
adminstrator and conductor, especially
of the Lower Rhine Music Festival in
Düsseldorf and the Leipzig Gewandhaus
Orchestra, Mendelssohn was responsible
for resurrecting buried treasures such
as Bach's Passions and B minor Mass,
and Handel's oratorios (on which he
modelled his own *St Paul* and *Elijah*).
He also helped to establish the role of
the conductor, and raise standards of
choral and orchestral performance.

In addition, Mendelssohn promoted
the careers of other composers and
performers, including Robert and
Clara Schumann, Berlioz, the violinists
Joseph Joachim, Ferdinand David
(1810–73) and Henri Vieuxtemps
(1820–81), and the pianist and
composer Anton Rubinstein
(1829–94). Many of his protégés
were invited by Mendelssohn to join
the staff of the newly opened Leipzig
Conservatory (inaugurated in 1843),
which under his direction became
one of the most respected musical
institutions in Europe.

*ABOVE: An Art Deco programme cover for
a dramatized pageant performance in
London in 1936 of the oratorio* Elijah
by Mendelssohn.

In 1837 he married Cécile
Jeanrenaud, daughter of a Lutheran
pastor. They had five children and their
marriage was happy but all too short:
Mendelssohn died of overwork and
grief in November 1847, aged only 38,
shortly after hearing of the death of his
beloved sister Fanny.

ABOVE: An annotated drawing made by Mendelssohn during his 1829 tour of Scotland.

Frédéric Chopin

*After playing Chopin, I feel as if I had been weeping over sins that I had never committed,
and mourning over tragedies that were not my own.*

OSCAR WILDE (1854–1900), "THE CRITIC AS ARTIST"

Chopin epitomizes the figure of the "Romantic artist": withdrawn, temperamental, talented and doomed to a premature death from tuberculosis. Like Paganini, he was both composer and performer (although his concert-giving was actually very limited), but his music established the piano as the 19th century's most popular instrument. He was also an important figure in the early nationalist movement, drawing inspiration from the folk idioms of his native Poland.

Born of mixed French and Polish parentage, Chopin began to compose before he was seven, and made his first public appearances as a pianist. On leaving school at 16 he enrolled at the Warsaw Conservatory, where he began to compose in earnest, and on graduating three years later he decided to seek his fortune abroad. In August

ABOVE: Frédéric Chopin (1810–49), painted by Albert Graefle.

1829 he made his debut in Vienna, playing two of his own piano works, including the set of Variations, Op. 2, whose publication Robert Schumann greeted with the immortal words, "Hats off, gentlemen, a genius!"

Polish themes

Chopin then returned to Warsaw, intending to leave soon afterwards on a European concert tour, but the tour was postponed owing to the volatile political situation and, meanwhile, Chopin fell in love. While he dallied in Warsaw, unwilling to leave, he worked simultaneously on two piano concertos. From his early youth he had been fascinated by the rhythms and melodic vitality of Polish folk music, and the finales of both concertos are strongly influenced by Polish dances — particularly the mazurka. After giving their premières with great success,

LEFT: An artist's impression of Chopin at the piano, composing his Preludes.

RIGHT: The monastery of Valldemosa on the island of Majorca, where Chopin and George Sand took refuge in 1838.

Chopin left Poland for Paris. On the way, he composed the great *Revolutionary* Study, in response to the devastating news that the Russians had captured Warsaw.

Paris

Chopin gave his first concert in Paris in February 1832. Although he was not a great success with the public, he was introduced to Parisian *salon* society, where his music was a triumph. From then onwards – although he rarely played in public – he became an instant celebrity. He was a sought-after teacher, consorted with the wealthy and powerful, and enjoyed the friendship of fellow composers (Liszt, Berlioz, Bellini and Meyerbeer), writers such as Heinrich Heine and Honoré de Balzac, and artists such as Eugène Delacroix.

Chopin also found lovers in this talented milieu – first the aristocratic singer Delfina Potocka, and then the writer Aurore Dudevant (George Sand), whom he met in 1836 at the home of Liszt's mistress. Their intense relationship lasted for nine years. They

ABOVE: Chopin playing the piano in Prince Radziwill's salon in Paris, painted in 1887 by Hendrik Siemiradzki.

spent the winter of 1838 in Majorca, hoping to reap the benefits of peace and a warm climate; but inclement weather and local hostility forced them to take refuge in the derelict monastery of Valldemosa. There Chopin finished his Twenty-four Preludes and other works, including the C sharp minor Scherzo. From then on he spent the winters in Paris and the summers at George Sand's country estate, but the affair finally fizzled out in 1847. By this time Chopin was seriously ill with consumption.

In 1848, Chopin was persuaded to visit England, where he played privately for fashionable social occasions. His last public appearance was at a charity concert for the benefit of Polish refugees. He died at his Paris home on 17 October 1849.

Chopin's music

Apart from the concertos and a handful of pieces for cello and flute, Chopin's output is all for solo piano. He borrowed the Irish composer John Field's new form, the nocturne, and raised it to fresh heights of subtle expression. His *études*, preludes, waltzes, impromptus and mazurkas were written to exploit and develop

piano technique; while the later polonaises, the *fantaisies*, the scherzos, ballades, the Barcarolle and the two sonatas, were all virtuoso works.

Contemporaries praised the "exquisite delicacy and liquid mellowness" of his tone, and the "pearly roundness of his passages of rapid articulation". These are still the hallmarks of great Chopin interpretation.

ABOVE: The writer Aurore Dudevant, alias George Sand (1804–76), Chopin's lover during the 1840s.

Life and works

NATIONALITY: Polish

BORN: Zelazowa Wola, near Warsaw, 1810; **DIED:** Paris, 1849

SPECIALIST GENRES: Solo piano music.

MAJOR WORKS: Two piano concertos; three sonatas; four scherzos; 25 preludes; 27 *études*; 19 nocturnes; 44 waltzes; ten polonaises; 56 mazurkas; four ballades.

Robert Schumann

To me, Schumann's memory is holy.
The noble, pure artist forever remains my ideal.

JOHANNES BRAHMS (1833–97)

Just as Mozart and Beethoven dominated the musical scene in the late 18th and early 19th centuries, Mendelssohn and Schumann were the standard-bearers until 1850. Schumann's personality and career exemplify musical Romanticism: his moody nature, fluctuating between exuberance and deep depression; his prolonged struggle to win the hand of his adored Clara; his receptiveness to literary stimuli, his obsession with numerology and secret ciphers, and finally his collapse into madness and early death, possibly as a result of syphilis (which, together with tuberculosis, put a premature end to many a flourishing Romantic talent).

Literary influences

Schumann was the youngest child of a bookseller, whose interest in literature

ABOVE: *Robert Schumann (1810–56), painted by Gustav Zerner.*

he clearly inherited. While still a schoolboy he began to compose music, and also to write articles and drama. He formed a society for the study of German literature, and in the novels of Jean Paul (pseudonym of Johann Paul Richter, 1763–1825) he found a role model for the two conflicting sides of his own personality, which he later characterized as Florestan (extrovert and impetuous) and Eusebius (dreamy, melancholic, introverted).

While studying law in Leipzig he began to take piano lessons with Friedrich Wieck, whose nine-year-old daughter Clara was showing extraordinarily precocious talent as a pianist. By now Schumann had decided to follow a career in music, but a hand injury (possibly a result of muscular weakness caused by mercury treatment

ABOVE: *The market-place at Zwickau, where Schumann was born.*

ABOVE: *Schumann's study at his home in Zwickau.*

for syphilis) put paid to his hopes of becoming a concert pianist. Instead, he decided to concentrate on composition and criticism.

Early works

By 1832 Schumann had published two major piano pieces: the *Abegg* Variations, based on a waltz theme derived from the name of a girl who had taken his fancy, and *Papillons* (*Butterflies*), a set of pieces linked by events at a masked ball described in a novel by Jean Paul. He also began work on a symphony.

In 1834 he founded the influential music periodical *Neue Leipziger Zeitschrift für Musik*, which he used to promote new musical talent, including Brahms and Chopin. He also used its pages to fight artistic philistinism by way of an imaginary society, the Davidsbund, or "League of David" (named after the vanquisher of

ABOVE: A romantic lithograph of Schumann composing his song-cycle Dichterliebe *(A Poet's Love).*

Goliath), whose members were given fanciful names: Schumann himself was either Florestan or Eusebius; Clara Wieck was Chiara or Chiarina; her father was Master Raro, and Mendelssohn was Felix Meritis. These names appeared in Schumann's set of 18 "characteristic pieces" for piano, *Davidsbündlertänze* (*Dances of the League of David*, 1837).

Marriage to Clara

In 1834 Schumann fell in love with Ernestine von Fricken, to whom he became secretly engaged (and for whom he wrote the set of piano pieces later titled *Carnaval*). When he discovered that she was only the illegitimate daughter of a Baron, he broke off the engagement and

Life and works

NATIONALITY: German

BORN: Zwickau, Saxony, 1810; DIED: Endenich, near Bonn, 1856

SPECIALIST GENRES: Songs, piano and orchestral works inspired by extra-musical impulses.

MAJOR WORKS: Piano music including *Carnaval* (1835), *Kinderszenen*, Fantasie in C and *Kreisleriana* (all 1838); about 250 songs, including song-cycles *Dichterliebe*, *Frauenliebe und -leben* (1840); four symphonies (No. 1 *Spring*, 1841, No. 3 *Rhenish*, 1850); Piano Concerto (1841–5).

RIGHT: Schumann composing at his piano. He had hoped to be a pianist, but was overshadowed by his more accomplished wife, Clara.

which overshadowed his own reputation as a composer), Clara stimulated her husband's creative imagination, acting as muse, confidant and critic.

Productive years

From 1840 onwards, almost in regular annual cycles, Schumann poured out song-cycles – including *Myrthen* (*Bridal Wreath*), his wedding present to Clara, *Liederkreis* ("song-cycle"), *Frauenliebe und -leben* (*Woman's Love and Life*), and *Dichterliebe* (*A Poet's Love*) – chamber music (including a piano quartet and quintet, and three piano trios), and a body of piano music unsurpassed by any other contemporary composer. It was Clara who encouraged Robert to try his hand at larger-scale works. These included concertos for piano (the popular A minor Concerto was written for her), violin and cello; four symphonies, and other symphonic works including the exuberant *Konzertstück* for four horns and orchestra and the *Manfred* overture, inspired by Byron.

Schumann's orchestral music has been criticized for heavy-handed orchestration (partly the result of his

ABOVE: Clara and Robert Schumann. Their marriage in 1840 marked the beginning of a partnership that was rare for its time.

transferred his affections to Clara Wieck, by now a delicate, dark-haired beauty of 15. Clara's father, who guarded his daughter jealously, was furious, and forbade Schumann to contact Clara. Then began an acrimonious six-year battle between Wieck – who made outrageous allegations against Schumann's character – and the lovers. Finally, in 1840, a court ruling paved the way for Schumann's marriage to Clara, which took place on 12 September.

Thus began one of the most remarkable musical marriages –

a partnership far ahead of its time – in which both husband and wife tried to combine family life with successful, independent careers. Clara Schumann (1819–96) was one of the most extraordinary women of her time. Her fragile appearance belied a steely inner strength, which enabled her to continue her demanding schedule of concert appearances all over Europe (she was one of the finest pianists of her age) while also coping with repeated pregnancies and child-rearing. While the marriage was not without its strains (Schumann resented his wife's success,

ABOVE: Clara Schumann (1819–96), photographed in middle age. She outlived her husband by 40 years.

ABOVE: An illustration to "Du bist wie eine Blume"("You are Like a Flower") from Myrthen, *Schumann's wedding present to Clara.*

own ineptitude as a conductor), but any defects are amply compensated for by its melodic charm and ingenious construction. Schumann's innovations include the recurring use of motto themes and other cyclical devices: in the D minor Symphony (No. 4), he directed that the thematically linked movements should be played without a break.

His large-scale vocal works include the secular oratorio *Das Paradies und die Peri* (1843), one opera, *Genoveva* (1850) and choral music including *Scenes from Goethe's "Faust"* (1853). As a composer of songs and piano music, he proved himself a worthy successor to Schubert. His piano music encapsulates an enigmatic private world, full of literary and musical allusions, autobiographical references and cryptograms: many of the piano pieces are built around references to Clara, such as the musical equivalents of the letters of her name. His songs include settings of Goethe, Adelbert von Chamisso (1781–1838), Eduard

Mörike (1804–75) and Joseph von Eichendorff (1788–1857), but his settings of Heinrich Heine (1797–1856), particularly the *Dichterliebe* cycle and some of the *Romanzen und Balladen*, are unsurpassed for their subtlety and lyricism.

Final years

In 1843 the Schumanns were reconciled with Friedrich Wieck, no doubt anxious to see his first grandchild. After a concert tour of Russia the following year they moved from Leipzig to Dresden. Schumann had always been prone to fits of deep depression and ill-health, and in 1846 he was so beset by nerves and chronic illness that he composed very little. By 1849 (when a revolutionary insurrection forced the family temporarily to flee Dresden), Schumann was becoming disillusioned by his failure to find a real job, and in 1850 he accepted an offer to become municipal music director in Düsseldorf.

His years in Düsseldorf were marked by failing health and mental instability, which adversely affected his abilities as

ABOVE: A page from the autograph manuscript of Schumann's Piano Sonata No. 3 in F minor, Op. 14, signed by the composer.

ABOVE: An illustration to Schumann's song "Der Nussbaum" ("The Walnut Tree"), No. 3 in the song-cycle Myrthen.

a conductor and caused increasing problems with his employers. He became obsessed with phenomena such as table-turning, and suffered aural and cerebral disturbances. Among the highlights of his later years were his meetings with the young Johannes Brahms, whom Schumann hailed in his magazine as a musician of the future, and the violinist Joachim, for whom Schumann wrote his Fantaisie for violin and orchestra and the Violin Concerto. Among his last compositions were the charming *Phantasiestücke* (*Fairy-tales*, 1849) for clarinet, viola and piano, and five Romances (1853) for cello and piano.

Schumann's mental faculties finally gave way completely in February 1854, and he began to experience hallucinations. After a failed suicide attempt, he was committed to an asylum. During the two and a half years in which he was incarcerated there, he was not allowed to see Clara. She was finally summoned to his bedside two days before his death on 29 July 1856.

Franz Liszt

I have not seen any musician in whom musical feeling ran, as in Liszt, into the very tips of the fingers and there streamed out immediately.

FELIX MENDELSSOHN (1809–47)

As a composer, Liszt tends to stand on the sidelines of music history, partly because he does not fall neatly into the German symphonic tradition, stretching from Beethoven and Schubert, through Schumann and Mendelssohn, to Brahms and Bruckner. But his influence on 19th-century music was enormous: he was a superlative performer (the pianistic equivalent of Paganini), an outstanding teacher, and a dedicated champion of the "music of the future", expressed both in his own innovative and highly individual work, and in his promotion of Wagner.

Liszt was the son of an official at the Hungarian court of Haydn's employer, Prince Nikolaus Esterházy. He showed prodigious talent as a pianist, giving his first piano recital at the age of nine, and Prince Nikolaus funded his education in Vienna, where he moved from an early age in aristocratic circles.

ABOVE: A portrait of Franz Liszt in old age, when he styled himself the "abbé Liszt"(Liszt the abbot).

Paris

In the 1820s the flamboyant young virtuoso began to cause a sensation in Paris (where his family moved) and London, where he played for King George IV. Back in Paris in the early 1830s he met Berlioz and Paganini, and made piano transcriptions of some of their works, including Paganini's Caprices, which in Liszt's version became the *Grandes études de Paganini*. He was also greatly influenced by Chopin's Romantic style.

In 1834 he began a liaison with the Countess Marie d'Agoult, which produced three children (their second daughter Cosima later married Wagner). They began a peripatetic existence in Switzerland and Italy, during which time Liszt compiled his *Années de pèlerinage* (*Years of Pilgrimage*) for piano, and the *Album d'un voyageur*.

LEFT: Liszt's summer residence on the corner of the Ilm Park in Weimar.

RIGHT: Title page of the score of Liszt's Hungarian Rhapsody No. 11.

By 1839 the relationship was under strain, and Liszt resumed his touring career as a virtuoso. He and the countess finally separated in 1844, and Liszt began a period of wild womanizing, which contrasted oddly with his secret desire to become a priest. In 1848 he became music director to the ducal court at Weimar, where he eventually settled with his new companion, Princess Carolyne Sayn-Wittgenstein (who was trying to obtain a divorce from her husband). She shared Liszt's interest in religion and mysticism, and encouraged him to write his most ambitious works.

Weimar

The Weimar years (1848–59) represent the zenith of Liszt's composing career. Most of his major works date from this period. They include two pieces inspired by the Faust legend – the *Faust Symphony* (based on Goethe) and

ABOVE: Liszt playing at a Parisian salon in 1840, painted by Joseph Danhauser. Listening (from left to right) are Alexandre Dumas, Victor Hugo, George Sand, Niccolò Paganini, Gioacchino Rossini and Countess Marie d'Agoult, Liszt's mistress.

Life and works

NATIONALITY: Hungarian

BORN: Raiding, 1811; **DIED:** Bayreuth, 1886

SPECIALIST GENRES: Tone-poems, programme symphonies, piano works.

MAJOR WORKS: *Années de pèlerinage* (1836–77); 19 *Hungarian Rhapsodies* (1846–85); piano concertos; *Funérailles* for solo piano (1849); tone-poems *Mazeppa, Tasso, Les préludes* and *Orpheus* (1851–4); Piano Sonata in B minor (1853); *Dante Symphony* (1856); *Faust Symphony* (1857); *Mephisto Waltz* No. 1 (1861).

Episodes from Lenau's "Faust" – the *Dante Symphony*; over a dozen symphonic poems inspired by literary or pictorial models, including *Tasso, Les préludes* (after a poem by Alphonse de Lamartine), *Mazeppa, Hamlet* and *Hunnenschlacht (The Battle of the Huns)*; the E flat Piano Concerto, the *Totentanz (Dance of Death)* for piano and orchestra, and piano works including the Transcendental Studies, the B minor Sonata, many of the Hungarian Rhapsodies, and the *Harmonies poétiques et religieuses*. In addition, Liszt championed works by other up-and-coming composers, giving the premières of operas by Wagner, Schumann, Berlioz, Verdi and Donizetti, among others. During his tenure, Weimar became known as the haven of the "New German School".

Holy orders

By 1860, however, Liszt had fallen out with conservative Weimar society (which disapproved of his open affair with Carolyne Sayn-Wittgenstein, and his promotion of "avant-garde" music).

He spent most of his later life in Rome, separated from the princess (who was never granted her divorce), and in 1865 he took minor holy orders.

A historian who saw him at the time described him as "Mephistopheles disguised as an abbé": his "diabolical" qualities, like Paganini's, were enhanced by his excessively tall, thin appearance, with long hair, originally blond, now white. He was still much sought-after as a teacher.

Liszt's later compositions are mostly sacred, and include the oratorios *Die Legende von der heilige Elisabeth (Legend of St Elisabeth*, 1857–62) and *Christus* (1862–7). However, they also include the Second and Third *Mephisto Waltzes*, one for orchestra (1880) and one for piano (1883). Among his last works – which became increasingly impressionistic in style – was *La lugubre gondola*, inspired by a premonition of his son-in-law Richard Wagner's death in Venice in 1882. Liszt himself died of pneumonia four years later in Bayreuth, having travelled there to attend the music festival.

Charles Gounod

A man has only a certain number of virtues, and all of Gounod's are concentrated on his art.

GEORGES BIZET (1838–75)

Gounod is remembered today chiefly for his opera *Faust*, based on Goethe's drama; and for the song "Ave Maria", an arrangement of his Meditation for violin on Bach's Prelude No. 1 in C. In fact, he was a prolific composer whose music was influential in both France and England.

Gounod's father was a painter and his mother a pianist. Like Berlioz, he studied at the Paris Conservatoire, winning the Prix de Rome in 1839. In Italy he fell under the spell of 16th-century polyphonic music, and began to write sacred music of his own (he also seriously considered becoming a priest). But he also met two influential women – the singer Pauline Viardot-Garcia (1821–1910), who introduced Gounod to the theatrical world, and Fanny Hensel (1805–47), who introduced him to her brother Felix Mendelssohn.

ABOVE: A scene from Goethe's Faust *– Faust tempted by Mephistopheles, painted in the mid 1820s by Eugène Delacroix.*

ABOVE: Charles Gounod (1818–93). His operas influenced Bizet and Tchaikovsky.

In 1843 Gounod visited the Mendelssohns in Leipzig, where he heard the famous Gewandhaus Orchestra, and music by Bach (then rarely performed).

Opera

On returning to Paris Gounod began to write grand operas in the currently fashionable style of Meyerbeer, together with elaborate masses and other church music. His opera *Faust* was performed at the Théâtre-Lyrique in 1859, and was an instant success: Gounod's gift for memorable tunes (such as the "Soldier's Chorus" and Marguerite's "Jewel Song"), and his subtle musical characterization of the doomed lovers, appealed to a Parisian

audience growing weary of Meyerbeerian bombast. None of his other operas (even *Roméo et Juliette*, 1867) was ever quite as successful.

England

Between 1870 and 1875 Gounod took refuge from the Franco-Prussian War in England, where his music appealed to Victorian sentimentality. Here, he acquired a ferocious English mistress, Georgina Weldon (he was chronically unfaithful), and founded the Gounod Choir, which eventually became the Royal Choral Society. In the 1880s he was preoccupied with composing oratorios (two of which were written for the Birmingham and Norwich festivals). Apart from the popular *Petite symphonie* for 10 wind instruments (1885), few of his later works have survived the test of time.

Life and works

NATIONALITY: French

BORN: Paris, 1818;
DIED: Paris, 1893

SPECIALIST GENRES: French grand opera, oratorios.

MAJOR WORKS: *Faust* (1859); *Roméo et Juliette* (1867); *La rédemption* (1881); *Mors et vita* (1884).

Georges Bizet

I am not made for the symphony; I need the theatre,
I can do nothing without it.

BIZET

Bizet's fame rests largely on just one work – the opera *Carmen* – but although his output was primarily operatic, several of his instrumental works, particularly the early Symphony in C, the suite *Jeux d'enfants* (*Children's Games*) and the incidental music to Alphonse Daudet's play *L'Arlésienne* (*The Girl from Arles*), have found a regular place in the repertoire.

Bizet studied at the Paris Conservatoire, winning many prizes, including the coveted Prix de Rome in 1857. Among his teachers was the opera composer Jacques Halévy, whose daughter he later married. The coolly classical Symphony in C was written at the age of 17, and in 1857 Bizet's one-act opera *Le docteur miracle* won joint first prize in a composition competition. He spent the years 1858–60 in Rome, where he picked up the chronic throat complaint which eventually killed him.

Life and works

NATIONALITY: French

BORN: Paris, 1838;
DIED: Bougival, 1875

SPECIALIST GENRES: Opera.

MAJOR WORKS: Symphony in C (1855); *Les pêcheurs de perles* (1863); *Jeux d'enfants* (1871); *Carmen* (1874).

ABOVE: Georges Bizet (1838–75), composer of the highly popular opera Carmen, *the tragic story of the life, loves and death of a gypsy. Bizet wrote* Carmen *towards the end of his short life.*

Early set-backs

In 1863 Bizet's first important opera, *Les pêcheurs de perles* (*The Pearl-fishers*), was put on at the Théâtre-Lyrique in Paris. It failed, although the famous duet from Act 1, "Au fond du temple saint", has always been a popular favourite. Afterwards Bizet was obliged to take up hack work from publishers in order to survive financially. Meanwhile he worked on several more operatic projects, none of which achieved success. The colourful Provençal background of Daudet's play *L'Arlésienne*, for which Bizet provided

incidental music in 1872, inspired him to find his true métier, and it was the similarly exotic setting and tragic story of Prosper Mérimée's *Carmen* which finally fired his imagination.

Carmen

Bizet's great opera was produced at the Opéra-Comique on 3 March 1875. It met with initial hostility, but within the next four years critics and audiences had come to appreciate the subtlety, power and originality of this vibrant score, and it was being performed all over Europe and in America. Bizet did not live to see its success. He died of a heart attack brought on by rheumatic fever on the night of its 33rd performance, just after the singer playing Carmen had fainted during the famous card-scene in which the gypsy heroine foretells her own death.

ABOVE: Célestine Galli-Marié, the first Carmen, who fainted on stage in the fortune-telling scene on the night Bizet died.

The Rise
✦ of ✦
Nationalism

A traditional Catalan festival held on Ash Wednesday to celebrate the beginning of Lent, painted in 1907 by Xavier Nogues (1873–1940).

The Nationalist Movement

The art of music above all other arts is the expression of the soul of a nation.

RALPH VAUGHAN WILLIAMS (1872–1958)

Up to the 19th century, music had been perceived as a common international language. Italian opera held sway in all European countries, as popular in Vienna, Stockholm, Madrid or London as in Venice or Rome; while the German symphonic style of Haydn, Mozart and Beethoven was adopted and copied by all European composers of their time. Only towards the middle of the 19th century did composers start to become aware of cultural differences between nations, an awareness prompted partly by political events, and partly through the Romantic cult of individualism, celebrating the unique qualities of both individuals and nations.

ABOVE: A Bohemian Landscape with Shepherds, *painted in 1841 by Ludwig Richter.*

Revolutions of 1848

The nationalist movement took root in central Europe, where in the 1830s a wave of nationalist sentiment swept through Germany, Poland, Belgium and northern Italy (at that time ruled by Austria). Over the next decade, the desire of autonomous states for political independence from the mighty empires that ruled them coincided with the democratic urge to replace monarchies with republican governments more in tune with the needs of ordinary citizens. This unstoppable force flared into violence in the year 1848, when patriotic sentiment and revolutionary fervour spread across France, Italy, Germany and central Europe. Although the revolutions failed, and autocratic rule tottered on in some countries until World War I, a new spirit of

LEFT: The Old Market-place in Prague, painted in 1865.

RIGHT: Mlle Eglantine's Dancing Girls — *a poster of the Belle Epoque in Paris, by Henri de Toulouse-Lautrec (1864–1901).*

nationalistic patriotism informed European politics from this time onwards, spreading into culture and the arts.

Folk music

In music, this patriotic fervour encouraged composers to seek inspiration in their national roots, particularly folk culture (often viciously suppressed by the ruling authorities). In beleaguered Poland, carved up by neighbouring powers after the Congress of Vienna, Chopin indicated his revolutionary sympathies by his use of Polish folk dances, especially the polonaise and the mazurka.

The nationalist movement was particularly strong in Russia (where Italian music – and Italian composers – had long reigned supreme at the cosmopolitan court in St Petersburg). Glinka was the first composer to draw inspiration from the distinctive melodic patterns and rhythms of Russian folk songs and dances, and his example was taken up with proselytizing zeal by Balakirev and his disciples, known as "The Mighty Handful", or "The Five". They in turn influenced Tchaikovsky, whose music, while not consciously "nationalistic", is still recognizably Russian in inspiration, drawing on folk legends and idioms, and epic tales from Russian history.

Landscape and people

The central European areas of Bohemia, Slovakia and Hungary, whose native culture had been suppressed by centuries of foreign domination, were particularly receptive to the new spirit of nationalism. The Bohemian composer Smetana was the first to celebrate the rich history and characteristic landscape of his native land in a series of tone-poems entitled *Má vlast* (*My Homeland*), and in a series

ABOVE: Spanish gypsy flamenco dancers, painted in 1898 by Ricardo Canals y Llambi (1876–1931).

of operas based on Czech subjects, from historical or mythical figures such as Libuše, to contemporary peasant life in *The Bartered Bride*. He in turn

ABOVE: The colourful costumes of 19th-century Russian ballet dancers.

influenced his pupil Dvořák, who effortlessly incorporated Czech song and dance idioms into European symphonic structures.

Nationalism was by no means confined to central Europe. Edvard Grieg, Norway's greatest composer, was trained in the German musical tradition, but his music draws plentifully on the folk idioms which he picked up on walking excursions into the Norwegian mountains.

In Spain, Albéniz and Granados exploited the colourful characteristics of Moorish-derived flamenco in their piano and orchestral works; in Austria, the talented Strauss family turned Vienna into the waltz capital of the world, and in England, then languishing under a dearth of native talent, the quintessentially "English" Savoy Operas of W. S. Gilbert and Arthur Sullivan exploited a rich vein of satirical English humour.

Mikhail Glinka

*I should like to unite in legitimate bonds the Russian popular song
with the good old Western fugue.*

GLINKA

Mikhail Glinka is regarded as the founding father of Russian nationalism in music. A contemporary of the Romantic poet Alexander Pushkin (1799–1837), he spent his early childhood with his grandmother, in whose care he first came into contact with the real music of Russia – the folk songs, pealing bells and ecclesiastical chants which would later inform his own music.

Glinka encountered Western music for the first time in his early teens, after he was sent to school in St Petersburg, where he studied violin and piano (including some lessons with John Field). On leaving school he became a minor civil servant, a job which left him plenty of time to indulge his passion for music as an enthusiastic amateur singer and pianist.

ABOVE: Mikhail Glinka (1804–57) working on his opera Ruslan and Lyudmila, *painted by Ilya Repin.*

Opera

He began to compose songs and chamber music in the 1820s, but a prolonged trip to Italy in the early 1830s left him with a passionate interest in opera. His own first opera, *A Life for the Tsar* – based on the patriotic story of a heroic Russian peasant who saves the tsar's life at the cost of his own – was written after his return to Russia, and proved hugely successful on its première in 1836.

Glinka found himself acclaimed as Russia's leading composer (although, to be fair, there was little competition), and encouraged by his success he immediately embarked on his next opera, *Ruslan and Lyudmila*. Unlike his earlier work, *Ruslan* was not well received. Its plot, based on Pushkin's fairy-tale (and involving such staging nightmares as a gigantic talking head), was cumbersome and ill-suited to the stage, and Glinka composed the score piecemeal. But its musical content – an appealing blend of elements drawn from Russian folk music, exotic orientalism and touches of "grotesquerie" – proved a rich legacy for all later Russian composers, as did his enthusiasm for the music of Spain (evinced in his two Spanish Overtures). Although Glinka died relatively young, his influence stretched far into the 20th century.

Life and works

NATIONALITY: Russian

BORN: Smolensk, 1804; **DIED:** Berlin, 1857

SPECIALIST GENRES: Opera and orchestral works in Russian nationalist style.

MAJOR WORKS: *Ivan Susanin* (*A Life for the Tsar*, 1836); *Ruslan and Lyudmila* (1842); Spanish overtures *Jota Aragonesa* (1845) and *Night in Madrid* (1848).

ABOVE: A cartoon of Mikhail Glinka by V. Samoilov (1853).

"The Mighty Handful"

Show me a people who have more songs!

NIKOLAY GOGOL (1809–52), "THE CONTEMPORARY"

This curious crowd of dedicated drinkers, who were largely amateur composers, was given its nickname ("moguchaya kuchka") by the critic Vladimir Stasov in 1867. Their self-styled leader was Balakirev, while Borodin worked as a chemist, Rimsky-Korsakov was a naval officer and César Cui was a military engineer, and the most gifted, Mussorgsky, was a civil servant whom the rest regarded with a certain contempt. Nevertheless, their influence on Russian music in the late 19th century was immense.

Mily Balakirev

Balakirev began piano lessons with his mother as a young child and

became a proficient pianist. While still quite young he came into contact with the music of Mikhail Glinka – one of his own earliest compositions was a piano fantasy on Glinka's opera *A Life for the Tsar*. Glinka imbued Balakirev with a strong sense of the importance of Russian nationalism, especially in music.

ABOVE:
Mily Balakirev (1837–1910), the driving force behind Russian musical nationalism.

RIGHT: The statue of Peter the Great in front of the Cathedral in St Petersburg (1844).

In the early 1860s Balakirev began to assemble a small band of like-minded disciples around him, and also played a major role in founding the Free School of Music in St Petersburg (he became its director in 1868). From this period date the beginnings of Balakirev's twin obsessions – collecting Russian folk music from far-flung regions and editing the works of other composers.

Balakirev was prone to fits of chronic illness and depression, and he was never a prolific composer. His single most frequently performed work is the ferociously difficult "oriental fantasy" for piano, *Islamey*. His main reputation was as an uncompromising critic of other composers' works. Tchaikovsky, among others, fell victim to Balakirev's stinging criticisms.

Of Balakirev's disciples, César Cui (1835–1918) was the least important. He wrote some 15 operas and other stage works, all of which have now disappeared from the repertoire.

Life and works

NATIONALITY: Russian

BORN: Nizny-Novgorod, 1837; **DIED:** St Petersburg, 1910

SPECIALIST GENRES: Romantic orchestral and piano works using Russian idioms.

MAJOR WORKS: *Overtures on Russian Themes* (1858, 1864); two symphonies; *Islamey* (1869); many other works for piano; symphonic poem *Tamara* (1882).

Alexander Borodin

Borodin wrote only one opera, but music from it is still a concert favourite. The illegitimate son of an elderly Russian prince, Borodin was brought up by his gentle, cultured mother, and showed an early interest in music. But his chief love was science, and he became a distinguished professor of chemistry, founding a School of Medicine for Women.

In 1862 Borodin met Balakirev, and immediately began work on a symphony. It was performed in 1867 with great success, and he started work on his second. Shortly afterwards, in 1870, he began work on the opera *Prince Igor*, whose composition dragged on over the next 17 years, and remained unfinished at his death. Although it was subsequently completed by Rimsky-Korsakov, it is rarely performed, but the exotic "Polovtsian Dances" which end Act II (in Rimsky-Korsakov's orchestration) have always been highly popular, as have the Second Symphony in B minor

ABOVE: *Alexander Borodin (1833–87), the composer of* Prince Igor, *one of the most colourful Russian nationalist operas.*

and the languorous Nocturne from the Second String Quartet. Many of Borodin's most famous tunes formed the basis of the 1953 musical *Kismet*.

Modest Mussorgsky

Arguably the most original composer of "The Five", Mussorgsky was bedevilled by mental instability, exacerbated by his heavy drinking. He showed an early talent for music, becoming a proficient pianist, but was destined for an army career. He completed his training and enlisted in the élite Preobrazhensky Regiment, but resigned his commission within two years. By then he had met Balakirev, with whom he began to study music seriously.

Financial difficulties then forced him to take a job in the civil service, while he continued to struggle with his first opera, *Salammbô*, based on Flaubert's novel. Although he started various projects with great enthusiasm, he finished few of them, and his three great operas – *Boris Godunov*, *Khovanshchina* (*The Khovansky Affair*) and *Sorochintskaya yarmarka* (*Sorochintsy Fair*) – were all left incomplete at his death (from alcoholic epilepsy), just after his 42nd birthday. He is also remembered

---

Life and works

NATIONALITY: Russian

BORN: St Petersburg, 1833;
DIED: St Petersburg, 1887

SPECIALIST GENRES:
Opera and orchestral works influenced by Russian and oriental idioms.

MAJOR WORKS: Symphony No. 2 in B minor (1877); *V srednei Azii* (*In the Steppes of Central Asia*, 1880); String Quartet No. 2 (1885); *Kniaz Igor* (*Prince Igor*, 1887).

ABOVE: *Russian folk dancers. All five composers in "The Mighty Handful" drew inspiration from their native folk music.*

Life and works

NATIONALITY: Russian

BORN: Karevo, 1839;
DIED: St Petersburg, 1881

SPECIALIST GENRES:
Opera in nationalistic idiom, piano works, songs.

MAJOR WORKS:
Boris Godunov (1872); *Khovanshchina* (1872–5); *Kartinki s vistavki* (*Pictures at an Exhibition*) for piano (1874); *Night on the Bare Mountain* (1877); songs; song-cycles.

ABOVE: Modest Petrovich Mussorgsky (1839–81), painted in the year of his death by Ilya Repin.

and his talent for orchestral colour, combined with exotic, oriental-sounding harmonies, produced many rich and glowing works including the *Capriccio espagnol* (*Spanish Caprice*), the symphonic suite *Sheherazade*, inspired by tales from the *Thousand and One Nights*, and the *Voskresenaya* (*Russian Easter Festival Overture*). This heady blend of Russian folk material and orientalism also informed the scores of many of his 15 operas.

Rimsky-Korsakov devoted as much time to his friends' work as to his own. He was responsible for orchestrating and completing, among others, Borodin's *Prince Igor*, and several works by Mussorgsky, including *Night on the Bare Mountain* and the operas *Boris Godunov* and *Khovanshchina*. Naturally he applied his own ripe orchestral palette to these works, and the modern trend in performance is to return as far as possible to the originals.

ABOVE: Nikolay Rimsky-Korsakov (1844–1908), one of the most popular Russian composers of his day.

for his orchestral piece *Ivanova noch na Lisoi gore* (*Night on the Bare Mountain*), inspired by a witches' sabbath, the famous *Kartinki s vistavki* (*Pictures at an Exhibition*) for piano, later orchestrated by Ravel, and his affecting song-cycles *Detskaya* (*The Nursery*, 1870), *Bez solntsa* (*Sunless*, 1874) and *Piesni i plyaski smerti* (*Songs and Dances of Death*, 1875–7).

Nikolay Rimsky-Korsakov

The most active and prominent of "The Mighty Handful" (and the youngest), Rimsky-Korsakov was born into a well-to-do naval and military family. He managed to combine a career as a naval officer with a productive sideline in composition. In 1871 he became professor of composition and instrumentation at the St Petersburg Conservatory.

Like his musical colleagues, he was deeply influenced by the nationalist work of Glinka, and he too fell under Balakirev's spell. Orchestration was Rimsky-Korsakov's great strength,

ABOVE: Sheherazade and the Sultan – a scene from the Russian Ballet version of Rimsky-Korsakov's Sheherazade.

Life and works

NATIONALITY: Russian

BORN: Tikhvin, near Novgorod, 1844; **DIED:** Liubensk, near St Petersburg, 1908

SPECIALIST GENRES: Operas based on Russian fairy-tales.

MAJOR WORKS: *Snegurochka* (*The Snow Maiden*, 1881); *Capriccio espagnol* (1887); *Sheherazade* Suite (1888); *Voskresenaya* Overture (1888); *Sadko* (1898); *Tsar Saltan* (1900); *Skazkanie o nevidimom gradie Kitezhe* (*The Tale of the Invisible City of Kitezh*, 1903–4); *Zolotoy Petushok* (*The Golden Cockerel*, 1906–7).

Pyotr Ilyich Tchaikovsky

Music is not illusion, but revelation.

Tchaikovsky could claim to be the world's most popular "classical" composer. His music has always held a special appeal, for its passion, lyricism, extravagant emotionalism, and glowing orchestral colour. It reflects the extremes of temperament of its composer – a moody, melancholy character, prone to fits of depression, but also of heightened optimism.

Throughout his life, Tchaikovsky was torn between his desire for a "normal" family life, and his homosexual nature. This constant, unhappy struggle was reflected in his music, particularly the later symphonies. Although associated with "The Mighty Handful", Tchaikovsky was never a member of that nationalist group. Much of his own work, however, draws on a rich vein of Russian folk culture, which he successfully fused with the Western symphonic tradition. He wrote: "As far as the Russian element in my music is

ABOVE: Pyotr Ilyich Tchaikovsky (1840–93), arguably the greatest and most popular Russian composer of the 19th century.

concerned, this is because I grew up in the provinces, imbued from earliest childhood with the indescribable beauty of the characteristic features of Russian folk music."

Early life

Tchaikovsky was the son of a mining engineer, and was born near the Urals. From his delicate, epileptic, French mother he inherited his hypersensitive nature and a tendency to hypochondria. When he was eight, the family moved to St Petersburg, where Tchaikovsky enrolled in the junior department of the School of Jurisprudence, a training-ground for the civil service. By this time, he had acquired twin younger brothers, Anatoly and Modest. He was exceptionally close to his mother, and her shocking death in a cholera epidemic when Tchaikovsky was 14 was a trauma from which he never really recovered.

LEFT: Tchaikovsky's father, Ilya Petrovich, with his twin sons Anatoly and Modest.

RIGHT: The square in front of the Mariinsky Theatre in St Petersburg in 1812.

Tchaikovsky graduated from the School of Jurisprudence in 1859, but found life in the civil service uncongenial. When a new music conservatory opened in St Petersburg in 1862, he enrolled as a student. He graduated in 1866, and found a job as a harmony teacher at the Moscow Conservatory, which had just been established by his mentor, the pianist and composer Nikolay Rubinstein (1835–81). The successful performance of an early overture in March 1866 encouraged him to start work on a symphony, entitled *Winter Daydreams*, which was performed under Rubinstein's baton in 1868. Modelled on Mendelssohn's *Italian* and *Scottish* Symphonies, it uses melodies influenced by Russian folk tunes.

Music for the stage

Meanwhile Tchaikovsky was working on his first opera, *Voyevoda*, which was performed at the Bolshoy Theatre in Moscow in February 1869. Shortly afterwards Tchaikovsky met Balakirev, who recognized a major new talent and

ABOVE: A page from the autograph piano reduction of Tchaikovsky's ballet Swan Lake *(1877). The score is a masterpiece and the ballet is a major part of the dance repertoire.*

ABOVE: The Swan Princess *by M. A. Vrubel (1867–1910), inspired by the heroine of* Swan Lake.

encouraged Tchaikovsky to tackle the tone-poem *Romeo and Juliet*. Its subject-matter, dealing with the favourite Russian themes of love and death, fired the composer's imagination, and it quickly became one of his most popular works.

In May 1872, while staying at the country estate of his beloved sister Alexandra and her family, Tchaikovsky wrote his Second Symphony, known as the *Little Russian*, which incorporates genuine Ukrainian folk tunes into its musical fabric. It was well received, but he still wanted to achieve operatic success. This eluded him until after his first venture into the world of ballet, with *Lebedino ozero* (*Swan Lake*), written for the Imperial Ballet in Moscow. Though its first production in 1877 was a disaster, it was the first of his three great ballet scores – the others are *Spyashchaya krasavitsa* (*The Sleeping Beauty*) and *Shchelkunchik* (*The Nutcracker*) – which are still the cornerstones of the classical ballet repertoire.

In 1874 Tchaikovsky's confidence received another severe dent when Nikolay Rubinstein contemptuously rejected his First Piano Concerto as "worthless and unplayable". Tchaikovsky rightly ignored the criticism, and refused to alter the score. After Hans von Bülow gave its première in Boston, USA, the following year with great success, Rubinstein was forced to admit his

Life and works

NATIONALITY: Russian

BORN: Kamsko-Votkinsk, 1840; DIED: St Petersburg, 1893

SPECIALIST GENRES: Symphonies, ballets, opera.

MAJOR WORKS: Symphonies No. 1–6; Piano Concerto No. 1; *Swan Lake* (1877); Violin Concerto (1878); *Eugene Onegin* (1879); *Manfred* Symphony (1886); *The Sleeping Beauty* (1889); *The Queen of Spades* (1890); *The Nutcracker* (1891–2).

ABOVE: *A scene from the 1993 Royal Ballet production of* The Nutcracker.

mistake. Meanwhile Tchaikovsky – who spent as much time as possible travelling outside Russia – saw Bizet's *Carmen* in Paris, and Wagner's *Ring* at the opening of the Bayreuth Festival Opera. Under these twin influences he composed his tone-poem *Francesca da Rimini* (1876), based on the famous episode in Dante's *Inferno*, and, in complete contrast, the classically poised *Rococo Variations* for cello and orchestra.

Marriage

Around the same time, he began his long association with the multi-millionairess Nadezhda von Meck, the widow of a railway tycoon, who befriended the composer, commissioned his works and supported him financially, on condition they should never meet. Her patronage enabled Tchaikovsky to concentrate on composition, and rescued him from the emotional chaos caused by his hasty and imprudent marriage in 1877 to a mentally unbalanced music student, Antonina Milyukova, who had pestered him with love-letters.

Tchaikovsky had evidently hoped that marriage would bring "normality" to his life, but found himself unable to reconcile his wife's physical demands with his homosexuality. An attempt at reconciliation brought him to the brink of suicide, and within weeks of the wedding he fled to the safety of his brother's house in St Petersburg. Tchaikovsky never saw his wife again, though they were never divorced. In

1896, three years after his death, she was declared insane and spent the rest of her life in an asylum.

Fatalism

In the immediate aftermath of his disastrous marriage, Tchaikovsky composed his Fourth Symphony, dedicated to Madame von Meck. He told her, "There is a programme to our symphony…the introduction is the seed of the whole work…this is Fate, the fatal force which prevents the realization of our hopes of happiness."

From then onwards, his work became increasingly dominated by the idea of Fate. It pervades his opera *Eugene Onegin*, based on Pushkin's verse novel, a powerful emotional drama set against the colourful background of Russian country life. The opera had uncanny parallels with Tchaikovsky's own situation, particularly in the ardent letter written by the heroine, Tatyana, to the insensitive Onegin, who fails to appreciate her true worth until many years later.

The same sense of predestination dominates the Fifth Symphony (1888), whose famous opening theme represents "complete resignation before Fate", while the second

ABOVE: *The Mariinsky Theatre in St Petersburg. Many operas and ballets by Tchaikovsky, including* The Sleeping Beauty *and* The Nutcracker, *were first performed there.*

ABOVE: *Tchaikovsky with his favourite nephew, "Bob" Davidov, son of the composer's beloved sister Alexandra.*

movement, with its exquisite opening horn solo, is a radiant love-song. Both Fate and Pushkin provided the scenario for Tchaikovsky's last successful opera *Pikovaya dama* (*The Queen of Spades*), a chilling supernatural tale of the death and destruction wrought by a gambler's obsession.

In 1878 Tchaikovsky resigned his teaching job at the Moscow Conservatory. From then onwards he spent much time abroad, in Switzerland, where he completed the Violin Concerto (another work strongly influenced by Russian folk themes), and in Italy (the inspiration of the *Capriccio italien* and the *Souvenir de Florence*). In 1880 he commemorated the historic defeat of Napoleon's army with the brash but ever-popular *1812* Overture, which he described as "loud and noisy…and probably artistically worthless".

By 1884 Tchaikovsky felt the need to settle down, and found himself a country house near Klin, outside Moscow. He renewed one acquaintance, with Balakirev (who

prompted him to compose the Byronic *Manfred* Symphony), but lost another when, in October 1890, his substitute mother-figure Madame von Meck abruptly discontinued their 14-year relationship.

Last years

The death of his sister in 1891 overshadowed an otherwise triumphant visit to the USA, and by the end of 1892 Tchaikovsky was beset by morbid fears. His last symphony, dubbed the *Pathétique* by his brother Modest, represents his final confrontation with the Fate that had dogged him. Tchaikovsky said that the symphony's "ultimate essence is Life", but that the anguished finale (marked *Adagio lamentoso*) represented Death. A week after its first performance on 28 October 1893, Tchaikovsky was dead, at 53.

The circumstances of his death remain a mystery. He is said to have died (like his mother) of cholera, after drinking a glass of unboiled water. Some scholars believe that

ABOVE: *A scene from the English National Ballet's 1999 production of* Swan Lake, *with Tamara Rojo and Patrick Armand.*

he committed suicide, either by drinking contaminated water deliberately or by taking arsenic, to avoid becoming embroiled in a homosexual scandal over a relationship with a public figure.

ABOVE: The Retreat from Moscow *by the Polish artist Jan van Chelminski (1851–1925). Napoleon's rout by the Russian army inspired Tchaikovsky's* 1812 Overture.

Bedřich Smetana

Here is a composer with a genuine Czech heart,
an artist by the Grace of God!

FRANZ LISZT (1811–86)

Nationalist feeling was particularly strong in 19th-century Bohemia, where Czech customs, culture, and even language were suppressed by its German-speaking Austrian rulers. Smetana was the first Czech composer openly to draw inspiration from national legends, history and landscape, and to incorporate the melodic patterns and rhythms of folk music into his work.

The son of a German-speaking master brewer, Smetana showed early promise as a pianist, and having studied in Prague and Plzen despite parental opposition, he decided to make music his career. He began by making a precarious living as a concert pianist and teacher, during which time he met the Schumanns and Liszt. In 1848 he took an active role in the unsuccessful Prague Revolution, helping to man the street barricades, and the following year he married a fellow pianist, Kateřina Kolářová.

ABOVE: Bedřich Smetana, influential in the central European nationalist movement.

Of their four daughters, three died in childhood, followed by the consumptive Kateřina herself in 1858. The family had spent much of the previous two years in Göteborg, Sweden, where Smetana had opened a music school, and where he had begun to compose symphonic tone-poems modelled on the works of Liszt, including *Richard III* and *Wallensteins Lager*, based on Schiller's play.

Czech nationalism

A few months after his wife's death, Smetana became engaged to his brother's sister-in-law, whom he married in 1860. He returned to Sweden that year, but events in his homeland were changing fast. The Austrians had suffered heavy defeats at the hands of Napoleon III's armies, and the time was ripe for a resurgence of Czech national feeling.

Smetana returned home early in 1861, hoping to become conductor

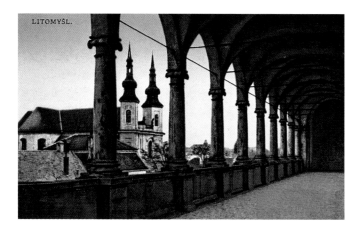

ABOVE: The Bohemian town of Litomyšl, where Smetana was born in 1824. Bohemia was part of the Austrian Empire at this time.

ABOVE: A view of Prague, showing the banks of the river Vltava, the inspiration for one of the movements in Má vlast *(My Homeland).*

of the new Prague Provisional Theatre, which had just opened for the performance of opera and drama, but having been raised as a German-speaker it took time to convince the authorities of his ambitions for Czech music. His first opera, *Braniboři v Čechách* (*The Brandenburgers in Bohemia*), with a libretto by the nationalist poet Karel Sabina, was produced there in January 1866 to great enthusiasm. It was quickly followed by *Prodaná nevěsta* (*The Bartered Bride*), which, with its appealing blend of rustic lyricism and the skilful incorporation of Czech dances, became Smetana's most popular opera.

Prague Provisional Theatre

In the autumn of 1866 Smetana was finally appointed conductor to the Provisional Theatre, where he introduced many major works to the repertoire, among them his own *Dalibor* (1868), based on a legendary Czech hero, and *Dvě vdovy* (*The Two Widows*, 1874). His most overtly patriotic work, *Libuše* (dealing with the legendary founder of the Czech ruling dynasty), was composed

ABOVE: Smetana at his piano, composing the opera The Bartered Bride *(1866).*

between 1869 and 1872, but had to wait until June 1881 for its première, at the triumphant opening of the National Theatre.

During the composition of *Libuše*, Smetana also worked on his great cycle of symphonic poems celebrating Czech history, legend and topography, entitled *Má vlast* (*My Homeland*). The most popular individual item has always been *Vltava*, a portrait of the river that runs through Prague.

Deafness and disability

In the early 1870s Smetana became aware that his health was deteriorating: he complained of giddiness and hearing problems (the result of syphilis). In October 1874 he went completely deaf in one ear. He was also suffering from financial problems, but nevertheless managed to complete a new opera, *Hubička* (*The Kiss*), in 1876. At the same time he wrote his E minor String Quartet, subtitled "From My Life",

whose last movement is dominated in the coda by a sustained high note representing the shrill whistling sound which Smetana suffered permanently as a result of his deafness.

Like Beethoven, Smetana continued to compose in spite of his disability. A seventh opera, *Tajemství* (*The Secret*, 1878), was followed by two new patriotic symphonic poems, *Tábor* (1878) and *Blaník* (1879), both inspired by episodes from Czech history. (*Tábor* is built around an early 15th-century Hussite chorale, effectively the Czech national anthem.)

Smetana's last opera, *Čertova stěna* (*The Devil's Wall*, 1882), took three years to write, during which time he complained of feeling as if he were standing "under a huge waterfall". He completed his Second String Quartet in March 1883, but his condition deteriorated and a year later he was taken to the Prague lunatic asylum, where he died on 12 May 1884.

Life and works

NATIONALITY: Czech

BORN: Litomyšl, 1824;
DIED: Prague, 1884

SPECIALIST GENRES:
Nationalistic Czech operatic and orchestral music.

MAJOR WORKS: *The Bartered Bride* (1866); *Má vlast* (1872–9); String Quartet No. 1 in E minor *From My Life* (1876); *The Kiss* (1876).

Antonín Dvořák

I should be glad if something occurred to me
as a main idea that occurs to Dvořák only by the way.

JOHANNES BRAHMS (1833–97)

Dvořák stands at the heart of the Czech nationalist musical movement. Like his contemporary Tchaikovsky, he succeeded in fusing folk idioms (the inflections of folk melodies and the characteristic rhythms of Czech dances such as the "furiant") with the symphonic techniques of his predecessors Beethoven and Brahms. His symphonies (particularly the three later ones), tone-poems, chamber and piano music are all part of the mainstream repertoire, and his operas (especially *Rusalka*, 1900) are becoming more widely known through frequent revivals.

Dvořák's father was the village butcher, and wanted his son to follow the same trade, but Antonín began to learn the violin at an early age and was eventually allowed to study music. He attended the Prague Organ School, and began his career as principal viola in the orchestra of the Provisional Theatre. He also began to compose and teach. He fell in love with a pupil, Josefina Čermáková, but when she rejected him he married her younger sister, Anna, in 1873.

By 1874 Dvořák had already completed four symphonies and two operas. That year he achieved his first real breakthrough when he entered several compositions in a competition intended to help struggling young artists. The jury included Brahms, who recognized Dvořák's talent, awarded him first prize, and took a fatherly interest in promoting his career.

ABOVE: Antonín Dvořák, the most famous Czech composer of his time. He was equally popular in England and the USA.

Brahms recommended Dvořák to his own publisher, who in 1878 commissioned a set of eight orchestral *Slavonic Dances* and within a year had published them, together with three *Slavonic Rhapsodies*, a Serenade for wind instruments, a String Sextet and Quartet, songs and piano duets. The infectiously tuneful *Slavonic Dances* in particular were a huge success, and assured Dvořák's international reputation.

England

From then on, Dvořák's works were performed as far afield as London and New York. In 1882 August Manns conducted the Sixth Symphony at the Crystal Palace in London, and the Stabat Mater was performed with great success in London the following year.

In 1884 Dvořák visited England for the first time, conducting some of his own works, including the Sixth Symphony and the *Scherzo capriccioso* for orchestra. He was immediately invited to write a new symphony (the Seventh, in D minor) for the Royal Philharmonic Society, and two large-scale choral works for the Birmingham and Leeds Festivals: the dramatic cantata *The Spectre's Bride* for Birmingham, and the oratorio *St Ludmila* for Leeds.

Life and works

NATIONALITY: Czech

BORN: Nelahozeves, 1841;
DIED: Prague, 1904

SPECIALIST GENRES: Opera, symphonies, tone-poems, chamber music.

MAJOR WORKS: Nine symphonies, including No. 9 *From the New World* (1893); Serenade for strings (1875); Stabat Mater (1877); *Slavonic Dances* (1878 and 1886); Requiem (1890); Cello Concerto in B minor (1895); operas; chamber music; piano music; songs.

London also saw the performance in 1887 of the *Symphonic Variations*, conducted by Hans Richter, and, in 1890, of the Eighth Symphony – often known as the *English*, although it is a thoroughly "Bohemian" work. The next year Dvořák received an honorary doctorate from Cambridge University.

America

In 1891 he was invited to become director of the new National Conservatory of Music in New York, at a very attractive salary. Dvořák spent five months touring Bohemia with several new works – including the Dumky Piano Trio and a cycle of three overtures, *V přírodě* (*In Nature's Realm*), *Carnaval* and *Othello* – before sailing for New York in spring 1892.

He spent three years there, teaching, conducting and composing. The Ninth Symphony (*From the New World*), the *American* String Quartet and Quintet, the Cello Concerto (whose coda reflects Dvořák's grief at hearing of the death of his sister-in-law Josefina), and the charming Violin Sonatina (dedicated to his six children) were all composed there. Several of these works show the influence of American folk music, especially the negro spiritual.

ABOVE: The National Theatre in Prague, opened on 18 November 1883. Dvořák's opera The Jacobin *was premièred there six years later.*

Return to Prague

The lure of his native Bohemia eventually proved too strong, and after 1895 Dvořák decided not to return to America. Instead he resumed teaching at the Prague Conservatory, and spent time with his family. The last decade of his life produced many new works, including two string quartets, four symphonic poems based on Czech folk tales – *Vodník* (*The Water Goblin*), *Zlatý kolovrat* (*The Golden Spinning-wheel*), *Polednice* (*The Noonday Witch*) and *Holoubek* (*The Wild Dove*), 1896–7 – and his two best-known operas, *Čert a Káča* (*Kate and the Devil*, 1899) and *Rusalka* (1900), both based on fairy-tales. He died on 1 May 1904, and had a state funeral.

LEFT: Dvořák with his wife and children, photographed shortly after their arrival in New York, 1892.

RIGHT: Dvořák conducting at the Chicago World Fair in 1893. The programme included the Eighth Symphony and three of the Slavonic Dances.

Edvard Grieg

I am sure my music has a taste of codfish in it.

GRIEG

Grieg was Dvořák's Scandinavian equivalent: a composer working outside the mainstream European symphonic tradition, though trained within it, who brought to his music a warmth and natural melodic facility that owed much to the folk music of his native land.

Grieg's father, Alexander, was a prosperous merchant of Scottish descent (the family name was originally Greig), who held the post of British Consul to the Norwegian port of Bergen. His mother, Gesine Hagerup, was an excellent pianist who undertook the musical education of her fourth child, Edvard, instilling in him a love for the music of Mozart, Weber and Chopin.

In 1858 the Grieg family was visited by the charismatic violinist Ole Bull, one of the pioneers of the fledgling Norwegian nationalist movement. Bull

ABOVE: *A portrait of Edvard Grieg (1843–1907), whose music epitomizes the scenic beauty of Norway.*

persuaded Grieg's parents to send him to the Leipzig Conservatory, where he studied piano with the composer and pianist Ignaz Moscheles (1794–1870) and composition with Carl Reinecke (1824–1910). He also heard Clara Schumann play her husband's Piano Concerto, which had an enormous influence on his own future concerto.

Norwegian music

Grieg began his career in Bergen, then went to Copenhagen. There he met his cousin and future wife, the singer Nina Hagerup, for whom he wrote many of his songs. His growing sympathy with the Norwegian nationalist movement dates from this period, when he met the young nationalist composer Rikard Nordraak. The two of them planned to found a society for the promotion of Norwegian music, but Nordraak died of tuberculosis. During the winter of

ABOVE: *Grieg with his wife Nina – the chief interpreter of his songs – photographed in 1906, not long before his death.*

ABOVE: *The autograph manuscript of Grieg's song* Fyremaal *(1880). Grieg often drew on Norwegian folk music for inspiration.*

1865–6 Grieg also visited Rome, where he met the playwright Henrik Ibsen. He married Nina in June 1867: their long partnership survived the death in infancy of their only child, Alexandra, and Grieg's later infidelities.

Grieg had already begun to write piano pieces with a national tinge (including the first of many sets of *Lyric Pieces*), but in 1868 his enthusiasm was aroused by his discovery of a volume of Norwegian folk songs. The influence of these mountain melodies spilled over into the Piano Concerto, which Liszt played through at sight when the Griegs visited him in Italy in 1869. On returning to Norway, and with Liszt's encouragement, Grieg determined to make a name for himself. He gave a concert of his own works (songs, piano pieces, and sonatas for piano and violin), and established an Academy of Music in the Norwegian capital, Christiania (now Oslo).

Peer Gynt

Grieg also began to collaborate with the playwright and poet Bjørnstjerne Bjørnson, director of the Christiania Theatre, on incidental music for his play *Sigurd Jorsalfar* (1872) and a

ABOVE: A Norwegian folk dance. The distinctive idioms of these dances, and the sounds made by Norwegian folk instruments, permeated all of Grieg's music.

potential opera. But it was Ibsen's request for incidental music to his play *Peer Gynt* in 1874 which fired Grieg's creative imagination. The resulting music, which includes "Morning", "In the Hall of the Mountain King" and "Solveig's Song", is well known from two orchestral suites, and rivals the Piano Concerto in popularity.

Troldhaugen

From the mid 1870s Grieg combined long European concert tours as a conductor and pianist with increasing periods of time spent in reflection and composition amid the beauty of the Norwegian mountains. He was particularly fond of the Hardanger district, where he composed in a small wooden hut by a lake. On frequent walking expeditions into the mountains he heard and collected folk songs and dances, whose idioms infuse his own piano pieces and songs, including the cycle *Haugtussa* (*The Mountain Maid*).

In 1884, the year he completed the anachronistic *Holberg* Suite for strings, based on 17th-century dances, he had a house built at Troldhaugen, above the Hardanger fjord near Bergen, where he entertained friends such as Percy Grainger. His much-loved home is celebrated in "Wedding Day at

Troldhaugen", included in the eighth book of *Lyric Pieces*, 1896.

By 1900 Grieg was suffering increasingly from lung disease. He was still much in demand internationally, and retained his life-long interest in his national folk music (his last works include a piano arrangement of Norwegian peasant fiddle tunes, called *Slåtter*). He died on the point of leaving for England on another concert tour, and his ashes were buried at Troldhaugen, in the side of the cliff overlooking the fjord.

ABOVE: The great Norwegian playwright Henrik Ibsen (1828–1906). At Ibsen's request, Grieg wrote incidental music for his play Peer Gynt *(1874).*

Arthur Sullivan

You ought to write a grand opera, Sir Arthur, you would do it so well.

Queen Victoria (1819–1901)

Arthur Sullivan was one of the most talented English composers of the 19th century, but he can only be described as a "nationalist" by default. In fact, he was impeccably trained in the German tradition. The son of a bandmaster, he won the first Mendelssohn Scholarship to the Royal Academy of Music in London, and went on to study at the Leipzig Conservatory, where he met Liszt and Grieg, before returning to England in 1861 to become a church organist. He was appointed Professor of Composition at the Royal Academy in 1866.

Savoy Operas

Sullivan was determined to succeed as a composer of serious and worthy music, particularly oratorio. But it was his meeting in 1871 with the

ABOVE: Sir Arthur Sullivan (1842–1900). He could never take his brilliantly successful "Savoy Operas" seriously.

playwright William Schwenk Gilbert (1836–1911) that ensured his lasting fame. Their first collaboration, *Thespis*, was a failure. But their second, *Trial by Jury* (1875), written at the instigation of the theatrical impresario Richard D'Oyly Carte, was a triumphant success. It was the first of a brilliant sequence known as the "Savoy Operas", operettas produced mostly at the Savoy Theatre in the Strand, London (which D'Oyly Carte – scenting huge profits – leased specially). Nearly all Gilbert and Sullivan's collaborations were resounding successes, *HMS Pinafore* running for 700 nights.

Composer and librettist were perfectly suited. Gilbert's hilariously witty librettos, parodying eminent British institutions such as the law, the

House of Commons, the police, the women's movement, the "Aesthetic" movement led by Oscar Wilde, and recognizable figures in public life, were perfectly matched by Sullivan's incomparable gift for musical parody (of Handel, Donizetti, Wagner, Verdi and others), allied with a gift for fluent melody and apt orchestration.

The partnership came under strain during *The Gondoliers*, and their last two operas, *Utopia Limited* (1893) and *The Grand Duke* (1896), were less successful. Sadly, Sullivan disparaged his own talents, rating his serious music, such as the grand opera *Ivanhoe*, much more highly. His assessment proved mistaken: the Savoy Operas have never lost their immense popularity, while the "serious" works have sunk without trace.

ABOVE: The cover of a piano arrangement by Bucalossi of songs from The Mikado, *inspired by the vogue for Orientalism.*

Life and works

NATIONALITY: British

BORN: London, 1842;
DIED: London, 1900

SPECIALIST GENRES: Operetta.

MAJOR WORKS: *The Sorcerer* (1877); *HMS Pinafore* (1878); *The Pirates of Penzance* (1879); *Patience* (1881); *Iolanthe* (1882); *Princess Ida* (1884); *The Mikado* (1885); *Ruddigore* (1887); *The Yeomen of the Guard* (1888); *The Gondoliers* (1889).

Jacques Offenbach

The opéra-bouffe is simply the sexual instinct expressed in melody.

NEW YORK TIMES, 1876

While the "Savoy Operas" of Gilbert and Sullivan took a wry look at Victorian England, France found its equivalent in the sparkling operettas of Jacques Offenbach.

Offenbach's German-Jewish family took their name from their home town of Offenbach-am-Main. His father Isaac was a cantor at a Cologne synagogue, who in 1833 took two of his sons, Julius and Jacques (by then a promising cellist), to Paris. Jacques was enrolled at the Conservatoire, but left after a year, and found a job in the orchestra at the Opéra-Comique. He also began to play in Paris salons, for which he wrote many pieces for cello and piano. During the 1840s he earned a living chiefly as a performer, and in 1850 he was appointed conductor at

ABOVE: Jacques Offenbach (1819–80). His operettas took Paris by storm in the late 1800s.

the Théâtre Français. In 1855 he rented the small Marigny theatre in the Champs-Elysées, where he put on a summer programme of short comic pieces. The success of this venture encouraged him to move to a more permanent venue at the Théâtre Comte, which he renamed the Bouffes-Parisiens.

Burlesque opera

Over the next 25 years Offenbach turned out over 90 stage works. His witty, light-hearted operettas satirized composers such as Wagner and Meyerbeer and captured the prevailing hedonistic spirit of Second Empire Paris, with its passion for music-hall dances and its relentless debunking of the Establishment.

In the mid 1870s his audiences began to tire of his productions and a run of expensive failures left him bankrupt, just at the time that Johann Strauss, whom Offenbach had encouraged to write operetta, was enjoying his greatest success with *Die Fledermaus*. Offenbach turned to a different kind of opera.

The Tales of Hoffmann

Offenbach's reputation also rests on his one more serious work, *Les contes d'Hoffmann*, which was left unfinished at his death. His supreme lyrical gift informs this tale of thwarted love, based on three stories by the Romantic author E. T. A. Hoffmann which are treated as episodes from his life. The "Giulietta" act, set in Venice, contains the "Barcarolle" which, together with the "Can-can" from *Orpheus*, ranks among the world's most famous melodies.

ABOVE: A can-can dance from Offenbach's La vie parisienne, *1866. Rossini called Offenbach "the Mozart of the Champs-Elysées".*

Life and works

NATIONALITY: German

BORN: Cologne, 1819;
DIED: Paris, 1880

SPECIALIST GENRES: French operetta and opéra-bouffe.

MAJOR WORKS: *Orphée aux enfers* (*Orpheus in the Underworld*, 1858); *Geneviève de Brabant* (1859); *La belle Hélène* (1864); *La vie parisienne* (1866); *La grande duchesse de Gérolstein* (1867); *La périchole* (1868); *Les contes d'Hoffmann* (1881).

"The Waltz Kings"

Where he fiddles, all dance – dance they must...

IGNAZ MOSCHELES (1794–1870)

If Sullivan personified Victorian England and Offenbach Second Empire Paris, 19th-century Vienna belonged to the Strauss family. Johann Strauss and his sons took the Austrian capital by storm with a torrent of light music – polkas, galops, quadrilles, marches, and particularly waltzes. In their hands the waltz, a sophisticated form of the Austrian *Ländler,* superseded its humble peasant origins to become the favoured dance of working-class dance halls and aristocratic ballrooms alike.

Johann Strauss the elder

The composer, conductor and violinist Johann Strauss (1804–49) was the son of an innkeeper of Hungarian-Jewish origin. A talented

ABOVE: Johann Strauss II, painted at the height of his fame in 1888 by August Eisenmenger (1830–1907).

violinist, he started out as the friend and partner of Josef Lanner, director of a popular dance orchestra. In 1825 they parted company and Strauss formed his own ensemble, which soon began playing at popular Viennese taverns. Within a few years the Strauss orchestra had been engaged to play in the dance hall at the fashionable Sperl Inn in the suburb of Leopoldstadt, a popular venue which attracted distinguished foreign visitors including Chopin, the young Richard Wagner, and the writer Hans Christian Andersen.

The repertoire of the Strauss orchestra ranged from dances, such as Strauss's own *Champagne Waltz* and *Sperl*

Festival Waltz, to fantasies on popular operatic airs of the time by Bellini, Auber, Rossini, Meyerbeer and others. Of Strauss's vast output, perhaps the best-known piece is the *Radetsky March* (1848).

From 1833 onwards the Strauss orchestra began to travel abroad, not only throughout Austria and Germany, but also to Paris and London, where it took part in Queen Victoria's coronation celebrations. Back in Vienna, Strauss was created Imperial Director of Court Dance Music. He had six children with his wife Anna (three of their

ABOVE: Johann Strauss I (1804–49) with his colleagues playing at a ball in Vienna.

ABOVE: The cover of a piano reduction of Strauss II's Promenade Quadrille.

ABOVE: Josef Strauss (1827–80), one of Johann II's younger brothers, also a talented musician.

sons carried on the family tradition), before leaving her to live with a mistress who bore him another seven offspring. He died, aged 45, of scarlet fever caught from one of his children.

Johann Strauss II

NATIONALITY: Austrian

BORN: Vienna, 1825; **DIED:** Vienna, 1899

SPECIALIST GENRES: Viennese dance music and operetta.

MAJOR WORKS: *Die Fledermaus* (1874); *Der Zigeunerbaron* (1885); waltzes, including *Morgenblätter* (*Morning Newspapers*, 1864), *An der schönen blauen Donau* (*The Blue Danube*, 1867), *Geschichten aus dem Wienerwald* (*Tales from the Vienna Woods*, 1868) and *Wein, Weib und Gesang* (*Wine, Woman and Song*, 1869); polkas, including *Tritsch-Tratsch* (1858) and *Unter Donner und Blitzen* (*Thunder and Lightning*, 1868).

Johann Strauss the younger

Strauss's eldest son, Johann, was known as "The Waltz King". He learnt the violin against his father's wishes, and in 1844 set up a rival orchestra that merged with the original Strauss band after the death of Johann I. Between 1856 and 1886 Strauss and his orchestra toured Europe, finding particular favour in St Petersburg, and also visited America.

His own compositions – waltzes, polkas, quadrilles and marches – were even more wildly acclaimed than his father's, and many of his waltzes are almost symphonic in scope. His works captured the hedonistic spirit of the Austro-Hungarian Empire at the height of its glory before World War I.

Strauss was also a talented composer for the theatre. Of his 18 light operas and ballets, the two outstanding works are *Die Fledermaus* (*The Bat*), an irresistible blend of Offenbachian wit and Viennese suavity; and *Der Zigeunerbaron* (*The Gypsy Baron*), in which Viennese Romanticism is spiced with Hungarian gypsy idioms. Both are still often performed.

Johann's younger brothers Josef (1827–80) and Eduard (1835–1916)

ABOVE: Eduard Strauss (1835–1916), the youngest of the Strauss brothers, pictured by a Vanity Fair cartoonist in 1895.

both shared in the direction of the Strauss family orchestra, and both wrote dance music of a similar kind, though neither achieved the same immense popularity as their father and elder brother.

ABOVE: The Viennese Ball *by Wilhelm Gause (1853–1916). The dance music of the Strauss family was the staple musical fare for such occasions.*

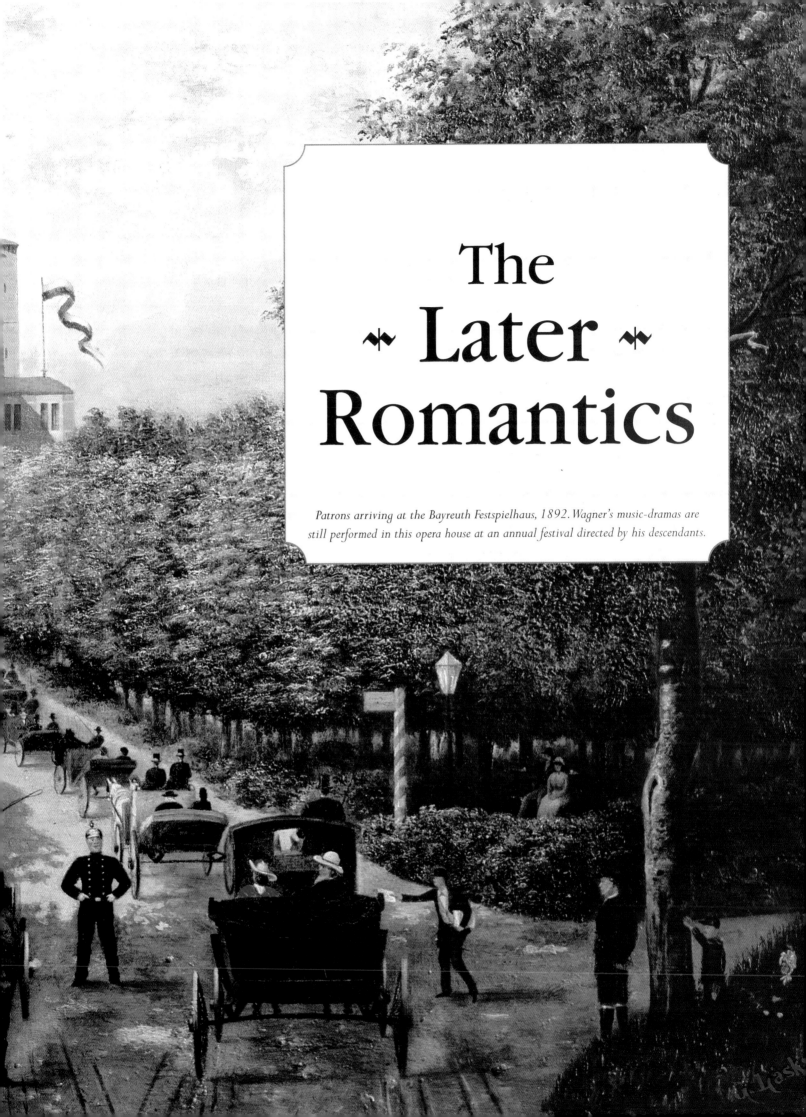

The ❧ Later ❧ Romantics

Patrons arriving at the Bayreuth Festspielhaus, 1892. Wagner's music-dramas are still performed in this opera house at an annual festival directed by his descendants.

Music on the Grand Scale

We are the music makers,
We are the dreamers of dreams.

<small>ARTHUR O'SHAUGHNESSY (1844–81)</small>

Two musical giants dominated the second half of the 19th century, each with a very different approach to composition. Johannes Brahms saw himself as belonging to the mainstream German symphonic tradition. Although overawed by the legacy of Beethoven, he – even more than Schumann or Mendelssohn – continued and expanded the Beethovenian principle of motivic construction. Brahms's four symphonies represent "pure", abstract music: unusually for a Romantic composer, they are unaffected by external influences such as literature or landscape. Brahms was primarily an instrumental composer. He wrote no opera, and his preferred media were orchestral, chamber and solo piano music. Yet, as his choral music and his many superb songs demonstrate, he was by no means indifferent to the power of words.

At the opposite pole stood the extraordinary figure of Richard

Wagner, whose works are almost entirely operatic. One of the most forceful and influential characters in music history, Wagner was highly receptive to influences of all descriptions – literature, myth,

ABOVE: The interior of the Teatro alla Scala, Milan; an aquatint from 1819. La Scala is one of the world's greatest opera houses.

LEFT: A snowy Finnish landscape – the inspiration for symphonies by Sibelius.

drama, poetry, painting, politics and philosophy. These combined to produce his "music of the future" – a vision of *Gesamtkunstwerk*, a "total art work", which would unite music, drama, poetry and the visual arts, and which he strove to achieve in his gigantic later operas, particularly the four constituents of the *Ring* cycle, *Tristan und Isolde*, *Parsifal* and *Die Meistersinger von Nürnberg*.

The operas and tone-poems of Richard Strauss owe an enormous debt to Wagner, as do the symphonies of Bruckner and Mahler (although both were equally influenced by Brahms). Wagner's influence was inescapable, and his genius so persuasive that the more unpleasant aspects of his personality – particularly the virulent anti-Semitism expressed in his polemical writings, which certainly contributed to the climate of opinion in Germany that led to Hitler's National Socialism – tend to have been overlooked.

Italian opera

Meanwhile, as in the early part of the century, Italian music continued to be dominated by opera, but in a very un-Wagnerian style. Giuseppe Verdi took on the mantle of Rossini, producing a sequence of 26 operas over some 57 years which have since remained the backbone of the international repertoire. Verdi was Wagner's only real rival in the operatic field, but his works are firmly based in the Italian *bel canto* tradition.

His successor, Giacomo Puccini, wrote far fewer works but almost all have held their place in the operatic canon. Puccini owed his success to an unerring sense of theatre and a persuasive melodic gift, allied to a taste for sentimental plots which still reduce

ABOVE: The Leipzig Opera House in the Augustusplatz, built between 1864 and 1867 (destroyed in World War II).

audiences to tears. In the hands of less talented composers, this taste for melodrama degenerated into the *verismo* school of sex and violence, which nonetheless produced two isolated masterpieces: the one-act *Cavalleria rusticana* (*Rustic Chivalry*, 1890) by Pietro Mascagni (1863–1945) and *I pagliacci* (*The Clowns*, 1892) by Ruggero Leoncavallo (1858–1919), which are usually performed together in a double-bill.

Nationalism

By the second half of the 19th century nationalism was in full swing and few composers remained untouched by an awareness of their national culture. Mahler in Austria, Sibelius in Finland, Fauré and Saint-Saëns in France, Elgar in England and Rachmaninov in Russia all made original contributions to the musical literature of their respective countries, broadly working with the language of late Romanticism.

All except Fauré were important symphonic writers, particularly Mahler and Sibelius. Elgar occupies a special place in British music as the most gifted English composer since Purcell. His music distilled the essence of Edwardian England, while Rachmaninov inherited Tchaikovsky's ability to write superb tunes, expressed with a passion that seems essentially "Russian".

ABOVE: The cover of The International Quadrille *by Charles d'Albert, showing the opening of the Crystal Palace in London in 1862. It became a favourite concert venue.*

ABOVE: Outside the Bayreuth Festspielhaus, 1892. The theatre was built in the 1870s specifically for performances of Wagner's music-dramas.

Johannes Brahms

I believe Johannes to be the true Apostle, who will also write Revelations.

ROBERT SCHUMANN (1810–56), IN A LETTER TO JOACHIM

One of the greatest symphonic composers of the 19th century, Brahms came from a relatively humble background. His father, Johann Jakob, played the double bass in the Hamburg city orchestra. His mother, who was 17 years older than her husband, came from a middle-class family who had fallen upon hard times: she had been Johann Brahms's housekeeper. Their second child Johannes was born on 7 May 1833.

Early years

Brahms learnt the piano from the age of seven, and from 1846 onwards he also studied composition. In 1848 he gave his first public recital, and that

ABOVE: Johannes Brahms (1833–97), painted by N. Piontkovsky.

year he also met the Hungarian violinist Eduard Reményi (1830–98), a refugee from Austrian oppression in his homeland. Five years later Reményi and Brahms set off on a concert tour, during which they met another Hungarian violinist, Joseph Joachim, and stayed at Weimar with Liszt. Brahms also travelled to Düsseldorf to visit Robert and Clara Schumann, who were both deeply impressed with the pianistic and compositional talents of this "young eagle", as Schumann described him.

Shortly after their meeting, Schumann suffered a complete breakdown, and in 1854 Brahms

returned to Düsseldorf to help Clara, with whom he fell deeply in love. Their relationship – whether physically consummated or not – was central to Brahms's life, and may have affected his attitude to other women: though he had close female friends, he never married. During her long widowhood, Clara acted as mentor to the young composer, encouraging him – as she had done with Schumann – to push his art to the limits.

In 1857 Brahms spent some months in Detmold, where he tried out his first orchestral works (two serenades) with the court orchestra. Two years later he settled back in

ABOVE: The influential Hungarian violinist Joseph Joachim (1831–1907), the dedicatee of Brahms's Violin Concerto.

ABOVE: A drawing of Brahms (aged 20) done at the request of Robert Schumann by Laurens, 1853.

Life and works

NATIONALITY: German

BORN: Hamburg, 1833;
DIED: Vienna, 1897

SPECIALIST GENRES:
German Romantic symphonies,
concertos, chamber music,
piano music, songs.

MAJOR WORKS: Four symphonies;
two piano concertos; *Ein
Deutsches Requiem* (1868); *Alto
Rhapsody* (1869); Violin Concerto
(1878); chamber and piano
works; about 200 songs.

Hamburg, where he founded a
women's choir and began to write
choral music. In the meantime he had
completed his First Piano Concerto,
begun at the time he met the

Schumanns. Brahms himself gave
the première of this huge work in
Hanover, where it met with success;
but five days later, in Leipzig, the
audience greeted it coolly. By this time
Brahms was making himself unpopular
by publicly dissociating himself from
Liszt and the "New German School".
His uncompromising stance probably
caused the Leipzig publisher Breitkopf
& Härtel to reject his manuscripts,
including the Piano Concerto.

Vienna

In 1862, with several more
compositions completed (including
the Sextet in B flat, and sets of piano
variations on themes by Handel and
Schumann), Brahms left Hamburg
for Vienna. Six months later he was
appointed director of the Vienna
Singakademie, where he indulged his
awakening interest in early music,
but he soon found the administrative
burden of the new job tiresome, and
resigned after a few months.

*ABOVE: Brahms in 1867, shortly before he
decided to move to Vienna, and one year
before he wrote the* German Requiem.

In 1864 he returned home on
hearing that his parents' marriage was
in trouble – his mother was ill and
his father resented having to look after
her. Their separation, followed by his

ABOVE: A Viennese street scene during the time of Brahms: the Fruit Market on the quayside near the Maria Theresa Bridge, 1895.

mother's death in January 1865, was a bitter blow (Brahms commemorated her death in the slow movement of his powerful Horn Trio).

In 1868 Brahms decided to settle permanently in Vienna, but continued playing his own works on frequent concert tours. In 1872 he became conductor of the Vienna Gesellschaftskonzerte, but held the post for only three years. A new breed of professional virtuoso conductors such as Hans Richter (1843–1916), Hans von Bülow (1830–94), and Hermann Levi (1839–1900) had arrived on the scene, and Brahms wisely realized his own limitations. In 1869 he had already had a taste of critical vitriol when Wagner (fearing a new and talented rival) had viciously

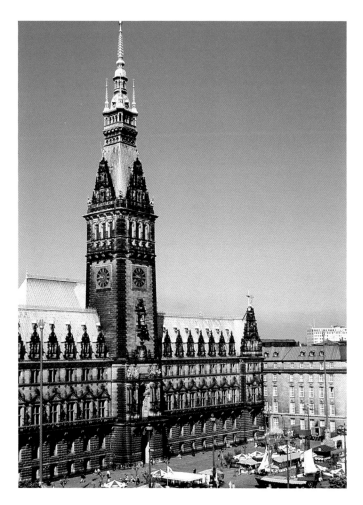

ABOVE: *The Town Hall in Hamburg, the city where Brahms was born in 1833.*

ABOVE: *The opening page of the autograph score of Brahms's Double Concerto for violin and cello (1887).*

attacked him in an article entitled "On Conducting". From then onwards, Brahms devoted himself to composition.

After many years of work, in 1868, Brahms had completed *Ein Deutsches Requiem* (*A German Requiem*) for soloists, chorus and orchestra – a deeply felt response to biblical passages on the subject of death, mourning and consolation – and during the Franco-Prussian War he was hailed as a "patriot", having used material from the Lutheran Bible rather than the traditional Latin text of the Catholic liturgy. He responded by composing the *Triumphlied* (*Song of Triumph*) in the summer of 1871 to celebrate Germany's victory. By 1873, when he finished his popular *St Anthony Variations* (*Variations on a*

Theme of Haydn) for orchestra, he was earning enough to be able to live on the income from his concerts and publications, and felt sufficiently secure to turn down a lifelong contract offered by the publisher Fritz Simrock (he also rejected an honorary doctorate offered by Cambridge University).

Symphonic success

Three years later, with Clara Schumann's constant encouragement, Brahms finally completed his First Symphony in C minor, begun over 20 years earlier. Its long gestation had been haunted by the ghost of Beethoven, and by Brahms's fear that the work would be rejected because it was not "programmatic". But the Viennese public received it with enthusiasm, and

ABOVE: *Brahms (centre) on the day of Clara Schumann's funeral, 20 May 1896. He had loved her ever since their first meeting.*

Brahms immediately began work on a second symphony.

In the late 1870s he adopted the habit of spending the summers in the Austrian countryside, at Pörtschach on Lake Wörther in Carinthia. There he completed the Second Symphony in D, the brilliant Violin Concerto (whose gypsy finale pays homage to Joachim, its Hungarian dedicatee), the G major Violin Sonata, the two Rhapsodies, Op. 79, and the eight Piano Pieces, Op. 76. From 1880 onwards he found another summer refuge at Bad Ischl, where he wrote the Piano Trio in C, the Quintets in F and G, the Three Motets, Op. 110, and many of his late chamber and vocal works.

In 1881 Brahms conducted his satirical *Akademische Festouvertüre* (*Academic Festival Overture*), based on students' songs, in Breslau, where the University had awarded him a doctorate. He did not care for honours, and failed to attend the degree ceremony. That year he completed the Second Piano Concerto in B flat – a *tour de force* of power and vitality, and a milestone of pianistic virtuosity. He also had a major disagreement with Joachim, who was intending to divorce his wife. Brahms took Frau Joachim's side, and the violinist broke off all relations with Brahms. (They were eventually reconciled in 1887, when Brahms wrote the Double Concerto for Joachim and the cellist Robert Hausmann.)

Also from 1881, the conductor Hans von Bülow – a great admirer of Brahms – offered the composer the use of the Meiningen court orchestra to try out his new works. These included the Third and Fourth Symphonies. The Third, in F,

ABOVE: Brahms at the piano – a posthumous sketch by Beckerath, 1899. Brahms had always been a fine pianist, having played since the age of seven.

was written in Wiesbaden in 1883, and the Fourth, in E minor, during two summer holidays in southern Austria, and performed on a European tour with the Meiningen Orchestra in the autumn of 1885. In its *passacaglia* finale, Brahms paid homage to another lifelong influence, that of J. S. Bach.

Last works

Brahms spent the following three summers at Hofstetten on Lake Thun, where he wrote his Second Cello Sonata in F major, two more violin sonatas, and the C minor Trio. By 1890 he had resolved to stop composing, but broke his resolution to write four clarinet works inspired by the brilliant playing of Richard Mühlfeld (1856–1907), principal clarinettist with the Meiningen Orchestra: the Clarinet Trio and Quintet and two clarinet sonatas. Clara Schumann's death in May 1896 prompted one final work – the *Vier ernste Gesänge* (*Four Serious Songs*) – but by then Brahms himself was mortally ill from liver cancer. He died on 3 April 1897, and was buried in Vienna's central cemetery.

ABOVE: The sixth book of Brahms's Collected Songs.

Anton Bruckner

Bruckner! He is my man!

RICHARD WAGNER (1813–83)

Bruckner's name is often coupled with Mahler's – but for no other reason than that both were Austrian and both wrote important, large-scale symphonies. In all other respects they were very different.

Bruckner's father was the village schoolmaster and organist at Ansfelden in central Austria. Anton, the eldest of five surviving children, was taught by his father, and by the age of ten was already a proficient organist. He also came into contact with the Catholic musical tradition at the nearby monastery of St Florian, where he enrolled as a chorister at the age of 13, after his father's death. St Florian was to remain the focus of Bruckner's life, and he chose to be buried there, beneath the organ.

Bruckner began his career as an ordinary schoolmaster in two

ABOVE: The Austrian composer Anton Bruckner – a portrait by H. Kaulback.

provincial villages. Eventually, in 1845, he returned as a teacher and then as organist to St Florian. His first important compositions, including a Requiem Mass and the *Missa solemnis* in B flat, date from his early years there.

By 1855 Bruckner had decided he wanted to become a professional musician. While working as organist at Linz Cathedral, he enrolled on a correspondence course in harmony and counterpoint at the Vienna Conservatory. He graduated in 1861 at the advanced age of 37, with glowing references. But he still felt he lacked musical knowledge, and sought further tuition in symphonic form and orchestration with the principal cellist and conductor at the Linz municipal theatre, who engaged him in a thorough study of Beethoven and Mendelssohn.

LEFT: A page from Bruckner's Ninth Symphony, left unfinished at his death.

RIGHT: The organ at the Abbey Church of St Florian. Bruckner was a chorister and then organist there, and is buried beneath the organ.

Life and works

NATIONALITY: Austrian

BORN: Ansfelden, 1824;
DIED: Vienna, 1896

SPECIALIST GENRES:
Symphonies, church music.

MAJOR WORKS: Nine
symphonies, including No. 4
(*The Romantic*, 1874–81),
No. 7 (1883), No. 8 (1885–90)
and No. 9 (unfinished,
1896); Te Deum (1884).

ABOVE: The Graben, one of the principal streets in Vienna, in Bruckner's time. Bruckner lived in Vienna from 1868 until his death.

The impact of Wagner

Up to this point, Bruckner had been competent but characterless as a composer. Then, in 1863, he heard Wagner's *Tannhäuser*, and the experience changed his life. Overwhelmed by Wagner's genius, Bruckner immediately began to try his own hand at symphonic composition. During the mid 1860s he attended many performances of Wagner's music, and even met the great man, while his budding confidence led to the composition of three masses and the Symphony No. 1 in C minor (1865–6).

After suffering a nervous breakdown brought on by intense overwork, Bruckner was eventually persuaded to apply for a professorship at the Vienna Conservatory, to which he was appointed in 1868. He also became organist at the Imperial Chapel in Vienna, and received a government grant to allow him to compose. He lived in Vienna until his death, leaving for occasional visits to Paris and London, where his organ recitals were greeted with huge acclaim.

In Vienna (where he was appointed a lecturer at the University in 1875) he devoted much of his energy to composing symphonies. Between 1871 and his death, he turned out eight more (No. 9 remained unfinished).

Despite Bruckner's growing fame, he encountered enormous opposition and hostility from two anti-Wagnerite sources. The Vienna Philharmonic Orchestra either rejected his symphonies as "unplayable" or deliberately sabotaged their performances, and the influential critic Eduard Hanslick — a supporter of

ABOVE: The beginning of the Gloria from Bruckner's Mass in D minor (1864), a page from the autograph score.

Brahms — took every opportunity to denounce Bruckner's symphonies, especially the Third (which Bruckner, in an enthusiastic fit of hero-worship, had unwisely dubbed his *Wagner Symphony*). Diffident by nature and fatally lacking in self-esteem, Bruckner also suffered from the interference of well-meaning but misguided "friends" who persuaded him to make cuts and alterations to the scores of his symphonies, in the interests of "accessibility". Many still exist in various hybrid versions.

Bruckner's first real success came at the age of 60, with the Leipzig première of his Seventh Symphony in 1884. He had finally found critical acceptance, although he continued to revise his scores obsessively. Official honours came his way during the last decade of his life. A simple, pious, old-fashioned man, he never married, although he proposed to a succession of astonished young women. He had a morbid obsession with dead bodies, and left instructions that his own should be embalmed.

Giuseppe Verdi

It may be a good thing to copy reality;
but to invent reality is much, much better.

VERDI, 1876

Verdi was the greatest Italian opera composer of the 19th century. Unlike Wagner, who strove to create a new type of music-drama, Verdi worked within the Italian tradition of his predecessors, but throughout his long career his technique became ever more fluent, his characterizations more rounded and expressive, and his response to the text increasingly refined.

His masterpieces are the Shakespearean operas *Otello* (1887) and *Falstaff* (1893), written when he was in his 70s, but works from all periods of his life form the backbone of the present-day operatic repertoire.

ABOVE: *Giuseppe Verdi (1813–1901), the greatest Italian opera composer of the 19th century.*

Early years

Verdi was born in Lombardy, at a small village in the vicinity of Parma. He began to play the keyboard when he was three, and at ten he was sent to study in Busseto. In 1831 he became the protégé of a music-loving merchant, Antonio Barezzi, who financed his further musical education privately in Milan, Verdi having been rejected by the Milan Conservatory. Verdi then returned to Busseto as the town's music director. In 1836, aged 22, he married Barezzi's daughter Margherita. They had two children, who both died in infancy.

In 1838 Verdi began work on his first opera, *Oberto*. He, his wife and baby son moved to Milan, where the opera had been accepted for production at La Scala. It was premièred in November 1839, a few weeks after his son's death, and in June 1840 Verdi's wife also died. During this sad period, Verdi was working on a new opera, the comedy *Un giorno di regno* (*King for a Day*), which failed utterly at its première at La Scala in September 1840.

Verdi was so discouraged that he almost gave up composing, but a friend persuaded him to begin work on *Nabucco*, based on the biblical story of Nebuchadnezzar. This — his earliest well-known work, famous for its chorus of Hebrew slaves "Va, pensiero" — was a triumphant

ABOVE: *The French dramatic soprano Rose Caron as Desdemona in Verdi's* Otello. *She created the role in 1894.*

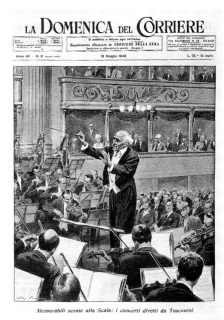

ABOVE: *Arturo Toscanini, one of the great Verdi interpreters, conducting the orchestra of La Scala Opera House in May 1946.*

ABOVE: A set design (c.1862) by Carlo Ferrario for Verdi's grand opera La forza del destino *(The Force of Destiny).*

ABOVE: A scene from a performance of Verdi's Aida *at the 1991 Savonlinna Opera Festival in Finland.*

success, and was soon being performed all over Europe. Before long, Verdi's name was being linked with the emerging nationalist movement in Italy, as choruses such as "Va, pensiero" and the Scottish exiles' lament from *Macbeth* (1847) were interpreted as coded rallying-cries for the oppressed Italian nation.

Galley years

With *Ernani* (1844), Verdi entered on a period he later called his "galley years", producing a string of operas for Rome, Milan, Naples, Venice, Florence, Trieste, and even London (*I masnadieri – The Brigands*, 1847). His early operas, up to *La battaglia di Legnano* (*The Battle of Legnano*, 1849), were still influenced by Rossini, and generally dealt with historical subjects (including the Shakespearean opera *Macbeth*).

Luisa Miller (1849) was the first of a series of works in which the subject-matter became more personal and intimate. The finest operas of this period are *Rigoletto* – the tragic tale of a hunchbacked court jester who seeks to avenge his daughter's seduction but inadvertently causes her death; *Il trovatore* (*The Troubadour*), another tragedy with the motif of revenge at its heart; and *La traviata* (*The Woman Gone Astray*), Verdi's version of *La dame aux camélias* by Alexandre Dumas. The

story of the courtesan who finds true love, sacrifices it for her lover's honour, and dies of consumption, is one of the most popular operas ever written.

Grand opera

Verdi's third period began with *Les vêpres siciliennes* (*The Sicilian Vespers*, Paris, 1855), and includes *Simon Boccanegra*, *Un ballo in maschera* (*A Masked Ball*), *La forza del destino* (*The Force of Destiny*, produced in

St Petersburg in 1862), *Don Carlos* (Paris) and *Aida* (Cairo). During this period he spent much time on the country estate he had bought near his birthplace, with his second wife, the soprano Giuseppina Strepponi (1815–97).

In 1861, after the Italian War of Independence, Verdi was elected to the new Italian parliament, and for the next four years mixed politics with composition. After *Aida*, he wrote little except his dramatic Requiem commemorating the death of the Italian nationalist poet Alessandro Manzoni (1785–1873).

Last works

The huge success of the Requiem prompted Verdi's publisher, Ricordi, to suggest a collaboration with the composer-librettist Arrigo Boito (1842–1918), on an opera based on Shakespeare's *Othello*. It took Verdi another decade to begin work on *Otello*, which with *Falstaff* marked the culmination of his career. His last work, in 1898, was a set of *Quatro pezzi sacri* (*Four Sacred Pieces*), including a Te Deum and Stabat Mater. By then Verdi had lost his beloved second wife, he was over 80 and worn out. He died in Milan in January 1901, leaving his fortune to a home for aged musicians which he had built in Milan, and which he regarded as "his greatest work".

Richard Wagner

Wagner's opera style recognizes only superlatives.

EDUARD HANSLICK (1825–1904)

The figure of Richard Wagner straddles the 19th century like a colossus. Composer, critic, polemicist, his abundant energy allowed him to a pursue a vision with a ruthless single-mindedness beyond the comprehension of ordinary mortals.

His operas, rooted in the German Romantic tradition, remain (like Verdi's) the cornerstones of the modern repertoire, but they require performers of extraordinary power and stamina. There are still few sopranos and tenors able to do justice to roles such as Siegfried, Brünnhilde, Tristan and Isolde, and many singers have burnt out their voices in the attempt.

ABOVE: An evocative portrait of Richard Wagner (1813–83), by Lenbach. Wagner was much given to striking romantic poses.

Early years

Friedrich Wagner died of typhus soon after his son Richard was born, and his mother Johanna married Ludwig Meyer, who introduced his stepson to the world of the theatre and music. The family moved to Dresden, where the young Wagner came into contact with Weber, then conductor at the Royal Theatre. According to Wagner, it was Weber who instilled in him "a passion for music". After his stepfather's death the family returned to Wagner's birthplace, Leipzig, where he completed his education at school and university. By now he was passionately

interested in the theatre, and in 1832 he began work on his first, abortive, opera. He realized from the start that he would only ever be able to work with his own librettos.

He began his theatrical career as a chorus-master in Würzburg, where he completed his first opera *Die Feen* (*The Fairies*). It remained unperformed, but already Wagner was showing a dogged determination to succeed. He began work on a third opera, *Das Liebesverbot* (*Love's Interdict*), based on Shakespeare's *Measure for Measure*, and joined a travelling theatre company as music director. *Das Liebesverbot* had a single performance in Magdeburg in 1836, before the company went bankrupt.

ABOVE: A costume design by Franz Gaul for the 1873 production of Wagner's early opera Rienzi *at the State Theatre in Brunswick.*

ABOVE: Senta leaps to her death — an Art Nouveau illustration of the final scene of The Flying Dutchman.

ABOVE: *A domestic vision of Wagner at home with his second wife Cosima, daughter of Franz Liszt.*

ABOVE: *A scene from the last act of* Rienzi, *premièred at the Dresden Hoftheater on 20 October 1842.*

By this time Wagner had fallen in love with the actress Minna Planer, whom he married on 24 November. Six months later Minna ran off with another man, but was reconciled with her husband in October 1837. Their relationship remained stormy.

Paris

Wagner was working at Riga (now in Latvia) when he began *Rienzi*. By March 1839, when his contract ended, he was heavily in debt (a *Leitmotif* of his career). He, Minna and their huge dog were obliged to flee from his creditors by ship to London.

In September they arrived in Paris, where Wagner hoped to establish himself as a composer. Instead he found himself trying to make ends meet from journalism, while financial problems landed him in a debtors' prison. He did, however, come into contact with a great deal of new music, and with literature, especially the Germanic legends of Tannhäuser and Lohengrin. His Paris period thus laid the foundations of several future operas, including *Der fliegende Holländer* (*The Flying Dutchman*), which he finished in 1841. The famous, storm-tossed overture to this dramatic tale,

of a restless ghost who is finally redeemed by faithful love, was inspired by Wagner's own experiences on the ship from Riga.

Dresden

In 1842 *Rienzi* was finally performed, with considerable success, at the Dresden court theatre, which agreed to mount *The Flying Dutchman* in January 1843. Although Wagner was

---

🎼 Life and works

NATIONALITY: German

BORN: Leipzig, 1813;
DIED: Venice, 1883

SPECIALIST GENRES: German Romantic opera and music-dramas.

MAJOR WORKS: *Der fliegende Holländer* (1841); *Tannhäuser* (1843); *Lohengrin* (1848); *Tristan und Isolde* (1859); *Die Meistersinger von Nürnberg* (1867); *Der Ring des Nibelungen* (1853–74); *Parsifal* (1882).

---

disappointed with the latter's reception, his career was finally launched, and he was offered the post of conductor in Dresden. In April 1843 he completed *Tannhäuser*, based on the legend of the knight – seduced from his duties by the pleasures of Venus – who is redeemed by a divine miracle. *Tannhäuser* was premièred in Dresden in October 1845.

Wagner began work on *Lohengrin*, which was finished in 1848, the year of revolution in Europe. Wagner's pro-revolutionary sympathies implicated him (by default) in the Dresden uprising of May 1849, and in fear of his life he escaped to Switzerland. He settled in Zurich, where he worked on his creative manifesto, *Opera and Drama*, and also began work on the texts of a new project, based on the ancient Nordic saga of the Nibelungs. *Lohengrin* could not now be produced in Dresden, so Wagner sent the score to Liszt, who had sufficient confidence in it to risk censure by mounting a production in Weimar in August 1850. It eventually became an outstanding success, although Wagner himself was unable to attend a performance until 1861.

ABOVE: A Romantic impression of Wagner composing his epic saga Der Ring des Nibelungen, *a cycle of four operas completed in 1874.*

Music of the future

Lohengrin – another legendary tale of knightly chivalry with a strong magical element – marked the end of Wagner's involvement with conventional German Romantic opera. In *Opera and Drama* he set out his visionary ideal of the "music of the future", in which music and drama became indivisible. The last 30 years of his life were dedicated to realizing this ideal.

By 1852 Wagner was again chronically in debt. He was helped by the merchant Otto Wesendonk, with whose wife, Mathilde, he fell in love. Their affair inspired the opera *Tristan und Isolde*, which Wagner began in 1857. This passionate portrayal of an adulterous love which can find fulfilment only in death is one of the supreme achievements of Western art. In it, Wagner pushed chromatic harmony to its limits, from the unresolved, "yearning" motif of the Prelude to the ecstatic dignity of Isolde's "Liebestod" ("love-death") in which she is finally united with Tristan as the strained "Tristan chord" achieves its radiant resolution.

Munich

Wagner's personal troubles continued. His wife discovered his liaison with Mathilde Wesendonk, and Wagner fled to Venice. With the police at his heels he moved on to Lucerne (where he finished *Tristan*) and then to Paris, where performances of *Tannhäuser* in 1861 were disrupted by an organized and noisy claque.

A political amnesty of 1860 allowed Wagner to return to Germany, but he spent the next three years travelling from city to city dodging his creditors, until a knight in shining armour appeared in the person of the "mad" King Ludwig II of Bavaria. Ludwig paid off Wagner's debts and offered him sanctuary in Munich, where *Tristan und Isolde* was first performed on 10 June 1865, under the baton of Hans von Bülow. Wagner repaid Bülow by beginning an affair with his wife Cosima (daughter of Liszt and the Countess Marie d'Agoult), who bore him two daughters, Isolde and Eva.

Wagner now had to leave Germany again in the face of Bavarian opposition to his powerful influence over the king and the vast sums of money that were being lavished on him from the public purse. Minna Wagner having died in 1866, Cosima von Bülow moved in with Wagner at his new home – financed by Ludwig – at Tribschen, outside Lucerne, where their son Siegfried was born in 1869. (This event inspired Wagner to compose the *Siegfried Idyll*, rehearsed in secret and played as a surprise for Cosima on Christmas morning.) After Cosima's divorce from Bülow, she and Wagner were married in 1870.

ABOVE: The Festspielhaus at Bayreuth, built to Wagner's specifications by Gottfried Semper between 1871 and 1876 for the performance of Wagnerian music-dramas.

Cosima – a formidable woman – kept Wagner on a short leash throughout their marriage, but protected his interests, and enabled him to compose in peace.

Bayreuth

In June 1868 *Die Meistersinger von Nürnberg* – a blend of comedy, philosophy, radiant young love and wisdom as embodied in the person of Hans Sachs the cobbler – had been premièred in Munich. At the same time, Wagner continued working on his *Ring* cycle, but realized that no existing theatre was suitable for such a large project. With King Ludwig's help, he raised the money to build a dedicated "Festival Theatre" at Bayreuth, where his operas are still performed at an annual festival directed by members of the Wagner family. The new theatre was inaugurated in August 1876 with three complete performances of the *Ring* cycle of four works – *Das Rheingold,*

ABOVE: A 1914 stage set for the "Garden of Enchantment" in Parsifal, *designed by Thomas Edwin Mostyn (1864–1930).*

Die Walküre, Siegfried and *Götterdämmerung* (*The Twilight of the Gods*).

Der Ring des Nibelungen – which contains over 12 hours of music – is held together by a complex system of musical references called *Leitmotifs*, in which characters and situations are identified by individual musical motifs, such as the joyous horn call associated with the hero Siegfried. By now Wagner's musical language had succeeded in merging voices and orchestra into one continuous texture, at the opposite end of the spectrum from the Italianate concept of opera as separate arias, ensembles and choruses. This complex, endlessly evolving web of sound proved an ideal vehicle for the grandiose Nibelung drama, which reaches its shattering conclusion as Valhalla burns and the world ends.

In 1882 Wagner finished his last opera, *Parsifal*, based on the quasi-religious myth of the quest for the Holy Grail, with its miraculous powers of healing. It was performed at Bayreuth in the summer of 1882, conducted by Hermann Levi. Wagner himself conducted the last scene of the final performance. Two weeks later, suffering from a heart condition, he took his family to Venice, where he died of a heart attack on 13 February 1883.

LEFT: Brünnhilde, from Arthur Rackham's 1910 watercolour illustrations to The Rhinegold *and the* Valkyrie.

RIGHT: The "Good Friday" scene from a 1950s Bayreuth production of Parsifal, *produced by Wagner's grandson Wieland.*

Gustav Mahler

To write a symphony is, for me, to construct a world.

MAHLER

Mahler was a transitional figure. A contemporary of Sigmund Freud and the painter Gustav Klimt, his massive orchestral works are rooted in the 19th-century Austro-German symphonic tradition and speak in a rich, late-Romantic idiom inflected with folk idioms, yet look forward to 20th-century preoccupations such as neurosis and mysticism. His most important works are his ten symphonies and his songs with orchestral accompaniment, which influenced them. Four of the symphonies – Nos. 2, 3, 4 and 8 – have substantial vocal and choral parts, which has tended to limit their performance potential, and for almost five decades after Mahler's death his works were largely neglected, admired

ABOVE: Gustav Mahler in the loggia of the Vienna Court Opera House, where he was conductor from 1897 until 1907.

only by a small band of devotees, until the advocacy of conductors such as Bruno Walter, Georg Solti and Rafael Kubelík in Europe, Leonard Bernstein in America and Norman del Mar in Britain, restored them to the repertoire.

Conducting

Mahler was born into a Jewish family and, although he later converted to Catholicism, his career was to some extent blighted by the anti-Semitic attitude of the Austrian establishment.

He showed musical promise as a child, and studied at the Vienna Conservatory from 1875–8, where he wrote the cantata *Das klagende Lied* (*The Song of Sorrow*). From 1880 onwards he made his living as a conductor at provincial theatres in Upper Austria, Slovenia, Bohemia, and then at Kassel in Germany, where he composed the song-cycle *Lieder eines fahrenden Gesellen* (*Songs of a Wayfarer*), and started his First Symphony.

In 1885 Mahler spent a year in Prague, and then moved to Leipzig. There he met the Weber family, who introduced him to the folk poetry collection *Des Knaben Wunderhorn* (*The Youth's Magic Horn*, published in 1805–8). From 1887 onwards he began to set some of the

ABOVE: Mahler's wife Alma with their daughters Maria and Anna, c.1906–7.

ABOVE: A page from the autograph score of Mahler's Sixth Symphony (1903–6).

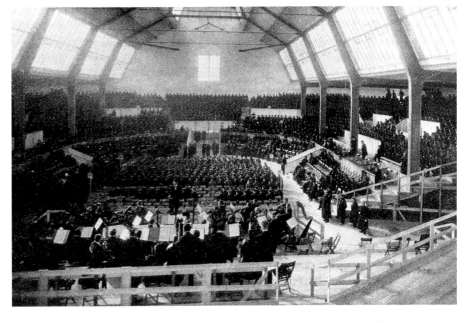

*ABOVE: Mahler rehearsing his Eighth Symphony (*Symphony of a Thousand*). The huge choir extends all around the auditorium.*

Wunderhorn poems, which were reworked in his earlier symphonies. Between 1888 and 1891 he worked as conductor of the Royal Opera in Budapest, before moving to the Stadttheater in Hamburg, where he conducted Wagner's *Tristan* in May 1891. By 1892 he had completed his First Symphony (first performed at Weimar in 1894), and had begun work on a second (the *Resurrection*). By then he had established a working pattern of conducting during the winter seasons, and retreating to the mountains to compose in the summer. The Third Symphony was finished in this way at Steinbach in the Salzkammergut.

Vienna

In 1897 Mahler was appointed conductor at the Vienna State Opera (one of his first productions there was Wagner's *Ring* cycle). He remained at Vienna for ten years, as one of the Opera's most distinguished music directors. In 1901 he found a new lakeside retreat at Maiernigg in Carinthia, where over the next few summers he composed the Fourth, Fifth,

Sixth and Seventh Symphonies, the *Rückert-Lieder*, the *Kindertotenlieder* (*Songs on the Death of Children*) and other works. The glorious *Adagietto* of the Fifth Symphony was an expression of his love for Alma Schindler, stepdaughter of the Viennese artist Carl Moll, whom Mahler married in 1902. Contrary to popular belief, the deeply affecting *Kindertotenlieder* pre-dated the death from scarlet fever of the couple's elder daughter Maria in 1907, although Alma believed that the cycle had "tempted providence".

ABOVE: The Metropolitan Opera House, New York, in the early 20th century. Mahler was appointed conductor there in 1908.

Mahler's Eighth Symphony (*Symphony of a Thousand*) dates from 1906–7. It was based on the text of a medieval hymn and the closing scene of Goethe's *Faust*, Part II. Mahler thought it "the greatest work I have yet composed". At the end of 1907, the victim of a vicious press campaign, he was obliged to resign his Vienna post, and also discovered that he had a potentially fatal heart condition. He was appointed conductor at the Metropolitan Opera House, New York, from January 1908, but continued to spend the summers in Europe, where he composed *Das Lied von der Erde* (*The Song of the Earth*), based on Chinese poems about the transience of life. He also completed his Ninth Symphony and began a Tenth.

In February 1911 Mahler became seriously ill, and died in Austria, aged 50. *Das Lied von der Erde* and the Ninth Symphony were given posthumous performances; the Tenth was completed in the 1960s by the British scholar Deryck Cooke.

Edward Elgar

Look out for this man's music;
he has something to say and knows how to say it.

HUBERT PARRY (1848–1918)

Like Arthur Sullivan (another composer knighted for his services to British music), Edward Elgar transcended the class barriers of his age, rising from humble origins to epitomize – in musical terms – Britain at the height of her Imperial glory.

Early life

He was born within sight of the Malvern Hills near Worcester, where his father ran a music shop and was organist at St George's Catholic Church. Edward's first job on leaving school was to help his father in both capacities, and he also began to play the violin in local orchestras and chamber groups. In the early 1880s he began to make a living as a freelance

ABOVE: Edward Elgar revived British music almost single-handedly.

player, teacher, conductor and self-taught composer with instrumental groups in the Malvern area. His composing ambitions were stimulated by his marriage in 1889 to his piano pupil Alice Roberts, daughter of a retired major-general. Alice, who was 40 when she married the 31-year-old Elgar, had social pretensions, and she persuaded her husband to move to London, where their only daughter, Carice, was born in September 1890.

Success as a composer at first eluded Elgar, and the following year the family moved back to Malvern, where he resumed his teaching activities and strove to overcome a sense of social inferiority. His persistence paid off when his overture *Froissart* was published.

Creative period

By the mid 1890s Elgar was becoming known for the cantatas he had composed for provincial festivals, including *The Black Knight* (1893) and *King Olaf* (1896), and in 1897 he finally achieved a breakthrough in London with the *Imperial March* for Queen Victoria's Diamond Jubilee.

In 1899 his first truly original composition, the orchestral *Enigma Variations*, was performed at St James's Hall in London. The Variations – each a

ABOVE: Elgar conducting in the studio in 1919, the year he wrote his Cello Concerto.

thinly disguised character portrait of a friend (including Elgar himself and his wife) – were recognized as a work of genius, while the underlying "enigma" – an unnamed tune which Elgar said "goes through and over the whole set" – has never been positively identified. The Variations encapsulate Elgar's musical style: noble, expansive, but tinged with plangent nostalgia for the English countryside.

In the autumn of 1899 the contralto Clara Butt sang Elgar's orchestral song-cycle *Sea Pictures* at the Norwich Festival, and he was commissioned to write an oratorio for the 1900 Birmingham Festival. The result was *The Dream of Gerontius*, based on a metaphysical Catholic text by Cardinal Henry Newman. Elgar was bitterly disappointed by the initial failure of this great work (which has since been recognized as a masterpiece), but the same year he was awarded an honorary doctorate by Cambridge University. His orchestral works were becoming popular, including the overture *Cockaigne*, inspired by London, and the first two *Pomp and Circumstance* Marches, of which the trio section from the first was later allied to the words of the verse "Land of Hope and Glory" written by A. C. Benson for the coronation of Edward VII. In 1904 Elgar was knighted.

The same year, the Elgars moved to a large house in Hereford, where over the next few years he wrote another oratorio (*The Kingdom*), the Introduction and Allegro for string orchestra (1905), and two symphonies. In 1910 Fritz Kreisler gave the première of Elgar's Violin Concerto,

ABOVE: *The programme for a gala performance at the Royal Opera House, 1902, in the presence of the new King Edward VII and Queen Alexandra, at which Elgar's* Coronation Ode *was performed.*

an eloquent work which bears an enigmatic dedication in Spanish: "Herein is enshrined the soul of…" This soul may have been that of John Everett Millais's daughter, Alice Stuart-Wortley, to whom Elgar seems to have been deeply attached.

In 1912 Elgar returned to London, to a grand house in Hampstead, where he wrote the cantata *The Music Makers* (1912) and the symphonic poem *Falstaff* (1913). He was greatly distressed by World War I, which he saw destroying the society in which his works were rooted, and his personal response was the elegiac Cello Concerto and three chamber works – a violin sonata, a string quartet and a piano quintet (all 1919). These were to be his last major works.

Post-war years

After Lady Elgar's death in 1920, Elgar wrote little more. He was created Master of the King's Music in 1924, and in 1932, the year the young Yehudi Menuhin made his historic recording of the Violin Concerto, the BBC commissioned a third symphony. Elgar was still working on it when he died of cancer on 23 February 1934. His wish that no one should "tinker" with it was respected for over 60 years, until it was completed by Anthony Payne (born 1936) and performed in 1997.

ABOVE: *Yehudi Menuhin (aged 16) recording Elgar's Violin Concerto in 1932, with the composer conducting.*

Jean Sibelius

Give me the loneliness either of the Finnish forest or of a big city.

SIBELIUS

The careers of Jean Sibelius and Edward Elgar have many parallels, although Sibelius, eight years Elgar's junior, outlived the English composer by more than 20 years. Each was responsible for a musical renaissance in his native land, and each developed a highly distinctive idiom, inspired to a certain extent by the musical characteristics of his native culture. Both composers lapsed into creative silence after middle age.

Sibelius was born into a Swedish-speaking family. His father, a doctor, died of cholera when Jean – who gallicized his given name, Johan – was still an infant, and the boy was brought up by his mother and grandmother. He was a promising violinist (he hoped to become a soloist), and was composing by the age of ten. From an early age he was much influenced by the *Kalevala*, the Finnish national epic, which – allied to an intense response to landscape and nature – was to provide the impetus for his own work.

ABOVE: A coloured drawing from 1904 of the Finnish composer Jean Sibelius (1865–1957) by Albert Edelfelt.

After leaving school Sibelius originally intended to study law, but gave it up in favour of music. In the 1880s he studied first in Helsinki,

and then in Berlin and Vienna, where he made many influential contacts, but also began the heavy drinking and financial irresponsibility which were to mar his later life.

Nationalism

Sibelius returned to Finland in 1891, where he worked on *Kullervo*, a symphonic poem for soprano, baritone, chorus and orchestra based on the *Kalevala*. Its immediate success established him as Finland's leading composer. In June 1892 he married the daughter of a Finnish nationalist general, thereby cementing his own identification with the nationalist movement (Finland was at that time part of the Russian Empire).

Although Sibelius never used actual folk tunes, his works of the 1890s are all distinctively Finnish. They include the four tone-poems based on the exploits of the legendary hero Lemminkäinen, of which the third is *Tuonelan joutsen* (*The Swan of Tuonela*); two more tone-poems –

ABOVE: A panoramic photograph of Helsinki, the capital of Finland, c.1910. Sibelius studied music at Helsinki's Conservatoire from 1886–8, where he became friends with the Italian/German composer Ferruccio Busoni (1866–1924) who was a member of the teaching staff.

ABOVE: *A photograph of Sibelius taken when he was a student in Vienna in his early 20s.*

En saga and *Skogsrået* (*The Wood-nymph*) – and the incidental music to *Karelia* (from which Sibelius made an orchestral suite). All these show the characteristic features of Sibelius's musical style, especially his liking for short motifs which are spun out symphonically, his use of *ostinato* patterns, and his effective handling of orchestration, with woodwind highlighted against an atmospheric string background, giving the impression of wind-blown open spaces.

Symphonies

In 1897 Sibelius – who was constantly in debt – was awarded a state pension which allowed him to concentrate on composing. Two years later he completed the tone-poem *Finlandia* and his First Symphony, clearly influenced by Tchaikovsky. It was followed by six more symphonies, written between 1902 and 1924, each of which is highly individual. The Second (1902) and the Fifth (1915) are perhaps the most popular (like Beethoven's, the Fifth is a "heroic" work); while the Fourth (1911) is compact and austere in tone, the Sixth more pastoral, and the short Seventh (originally called *Fantasia sinfonica*) is in a single movement. An Eighth Symphony was written, but immediately destroyed.

During the early years of the 20th century, Sibelius travelled extensively, visiting England, Bohemia and Italy. The Violin Concerto dates from 1903, a period in which Sibelius's drinking and debt put his marriage under strain. In 1904 he built himself a villa outside Helsinki, where he lived for the rest of his life. The tone-poems *Pohjolan tytär* (*Pohjola's Daughter*) and *Oinen ratsastus ja auringonnousu* (*Night-ride and Sunrise*) date from this period, as does the

Life and works

NATIONALITY: Finnish

BORN: Hämeenlinna, 1865; DIED: Järvanpää, 1957

SPECIALIST GENRES: Symphonies.

MAJOR WORKS: Seven symphonies; *En saga* (1892–1902); *Lemminkäinen Legends* (1893–7); *Karelia Suite* (1893); *Finlandia* (1899); Violin Concerto (1903–5).

incidental music to Maurice Maeterlinck's *Pelléas et Mélisande* (a play which Debussy used as the basis for his opera) and *Belsazars gästabud* (*Belshazzar's Feast*, a Biblical episode later set by William Walton).

Silence

In 1908 Sibelius underwent an operation for suspected throat cancer, and his later works have an intensified bleakness. He continued to travel throughout Europe and to America to conduct his works until the outbreak of World War I, an event which virtually ended his creative life. After the war he wrote only four more major pieces, including incidental music for Shakespeare's *The Tempest* (1925), and his last symphonic poem, *Tapiola* (1926). For the remaining 31 years of his life, he composed nothing, disliked talking about his music and became increasingly reclusive.

ABOVE: *An impressionistic illustration of Sibelius's tone-poem* The Swan of Tuonela *(1893–7) by I. J. Belmont.*

Camille Saint-Saëns

There is nothing more difficult than talking about music.

SAINT-SAËNS

The French composer Camille Saint-Saëns was, like Mozart and Mendelssohn, a child prodigy. His father died just after he was born, and he was brought up by his mother and an aunt who began to teach him the piano when he was two. He was composing by the age of three, and played concertos by Mozart and Beethoven when he was ten. He also showed a keen interest in other intellectual pursuits, particularly archaeology, geology, astronomy and philosophy.

Saint-Saëns studied at the Paris Conservatoire, and was organist at the Madeleine church in Paris from 1857–76. After hearing him improvise, Liszt declared him the greatest organist in the world. In return, Saint-Saëns acknowledged Liszt's influence on his own symphonic poems of the 1870s: *Le rouet d'Omphale* (*Omphale's Spinning Wheel*), *Phaëton*, the enormously popular *Danse macabre*, and *La jeunesse d'Hercule* (*Hercules' Youth*). In 1871 he was a founder-member of the Société Nationale de Musique, set up to promote performances of works by younger French composers.

ABOVE: Camille Saint-Saëns (1835–1921). He was an amazingly prolific composer — "I compose music as a tree produces apples", he said.

Saint-Saëns was much attached to his mother but, much to her disapproval, when he was 40 he married a girl half his age. Their two young sons died tragically within six weeks of each other, and after just six years of marriage, Saint-Saëns walked out on his wife. After his mother's death in 1888 he spent much time abroad, especially in North Africa, and many of his works, such as the Fifth Piano Concerto, make use of exotic harmonies.

His most famous and enduring works include the opera *Samson et Dalila*, the First Cello Concerto, the Introduction and Rondo Capriccioso for violin and orchestra, the five piano concertos, the Organ Symphony (No. 3), and *Le carnaval des animaux* (*The Carnival of the Animals*), written as a private joke for performance by friends.

LEFT: The entrance to the Paris Conservatoire de Musique et de Déclamation in the rue Bergère, where Saint-Saëns studied.

Life and works

NATIONALITY: French

BORN: Paris, 1835; **DIED:** Algiers, 1921

SPECIALIST GENRES: Tone-poems, piano concertos.

MAJOR WORKS: Piano Concerto No. 2 (1868); Cello Concerto No. 1 (1873); *Danse macabre* (1874); *Samson et Dalila* (1877); Symphony No. 3 (1886); *Le carnaval des animaux* (1886).

Gabriel Fauré

For me…music exists to elevate us as far as possible above everyday existence.

Fauré, in a letter to his son Philippe, 1908

Fauré was Saint-Saëns' favourite pupil at the Ecole Niedermeyer in Paris. Like his teacher, he was a gifted pianist and organist, and began his career as an organist in Rennes. In 1871 he became organist at Ste Sulpice in Paris, and was also active in the foundation of the Société Nationale de Musique, where many of his own works were given their premières.

Fauré's engagement to Marianne Viardot (the daughter of a famous singer) produced three fine chamber works: the First Violin Sonata, the First Piano Quartet, and the Ballade for piano. In 1882, five years after Marianne broke off the engagement, he married Marie Fremiet, the daughter of a sculptor. The marriage, which produced two sons, was unhappy, and Fauré found consolation with other women, including Emma Bardac (the

ABOVE: Gabriel Fauré (1845–1924), aged 18. He studied with Saint-Saëns, and later taught at the Paris Conservatoire.

second Mme Debussy), for whom he wrote the tender song-cycle *La bonne chanson*, and for whose daughter Hélène (nicknamed Dolly) he wrote the *Dolly* Suite for piano duet.

Fauré continued to earn a living as organist, choir-master and teacher, and was able to compose only in his spare time. He was happiest with small-scale genres such as songs, piano and chamber music: many of his delicate, elusive songs are settings of texts by the Symbolist poet Paul Verlaine. His famous Requiem – probably his best-known work – took over 20 years to finish. In the late 1890s he was appointed principal organist of the Madeleine church in Paris, and also

became a professor of composition at the Paris Conservatoire, where his pupils included Ravel. He became director of the Conservatoire in 1905.

By the age of 50 Fauré was well-known in Parisian society (his friends included Marcel Proust). By this time he was attempting larger-scale works, including the incidental music to Maeterlinck's play *Pelléas et Mélisande* (which also inspired Debussy and Sibelius), the orchestral suite in 18th-century style *Masques et bergamasques* (1919) and the stage works *Prométhée* and *Pénélope*.

He retired from the Conservatoire in 1920, and was finally able to devote himself to composition, although by this time he was losing his hearing. His late works were mostly for chamber combinations, including a Piano Trio and Piano Quintet.

ABOVE: Fauré playing the organ at the Church of the Madeleine in Paris, where he was principal organist for many years.

Life and works

NATIONALITY: French

BORN: Pamiers, Ariège, 1845; **DIED:** Paris, 1924

SPECIALIST GENRES: Songs, piano and chamber music.

MAJOR WORKS: Songs and song-cycles; piano music, including *Dolly* Suite (1897); *Pavane* (1887); Requiem (1888); *Pelléas et Mélisande* (1892); *Pénélope* (1913).

Giacomo Puccini

*I shall feel it [the story of Manon] as an Italian,
with desperate passion.*

PUCCINI

Puccini was the last great exponent of Italian Romantic opera. His operas have always held a special place in the affections of audiences, and rival Verdi's in popularity. He was born into a dynasty of musicians who since the 18th century had been organists at the church of San Martino in Lucca. It had been intended that Puccini should follow the family tradition, but seeing a performance of Verdi's *Aida* at Pisa made him decide to become an opera composer.

Milan

In 1880 a scholarship enabled Puccini to enrol at the Milan Conservatory. He graduated in the summer of 1883, having entered a one-act opera, *Le villi* (*The Witches*), in a competition sponsored by a music publisher. It came nowhere, but the next year Puccini played it through at a party attended by Verdi's publisher Ricordi. *Le villi* was staged in 1884, and

ABOVE: A portrait of Giacomo Puccini (1858–1924) painted in Paris in 1899, three years after he wrote his highly popular opera La Bohème.

Ricordi immediately commissioned another opera, *Edgar*, from the young composer, and signed him up.

Edgar was performed at La Scala in Milan in 1889, but was not well received (the composer himself described it as a "mistake"). But his next opera, *Manon Lescaut* (based, like Massenet's opera *Manon*, on the novel by Abbé Prévost), was a huge success at its Turin première in 1893. Puccini had found a winning formula: that of the young, doomed heroine whose flawed character leads to an affecting early death. He repeated it with *La Bohème* (*The Bohemian Girl*), first performed at Turin in 1896 under Toscanini; but it took some time for this romantic drama of love and death in a Montmartre garret – now one of the world's most popular operas – to catch the public's imagination.

Puccini's next opera, *Tosca*, performed in Rome in 1900, was an excursion into the brutal world of *verismo*. Its

ABOVE: Puccini at home in the music-room of his villa at Torre del Lago, near Lucca.

ABOVE: A stage set for Act I of Puccini's Tosca, *set in the Roman church of S Andrea delle Valle.*

"body count" – an attempted rape, a murder, a faked execution by firing squad which turns out to be real, and a final, dramatic suicide – has rarely been surpassed. Critics have always been snooty about *Tosca* (one described it memorably as "a shabby little shocker"), but Puccini's marvellous melodic gift and innate sense of drama save it from mere sensationalism.

Based on a real-life incident, as related in David Belasco's play, *Madama Butterfly* (La Scala, 1904) returned to the "weepie" genre. The tragic tale of a Japanese geisha, betrayed and abandoned by the American naval lieutenant she believes to be her husband, took the operatic world by storm after Puccini revised it into three acts. Another Belasco play, *The Girl of the Golden West*, provided the subject-matter for Puccini's next opera, *La fanciulla del West*, premièred at the New York Metropolitan Opera in December 1910 with Enrico Caruso and Emmy Destinn in the leading roles.

Puccini made a political mistake with his next opera, accepting a commission from the directors of a Viennese theatre instead of an Italian one,

ABOVE: A poster for the original 1904 production of Madama Butterfly. *Butterfly is shown bidding farewell to her child before killing herself.*

drawing accusations of treachery. The little-known *La rondine* (*The Swallow*) was first performed during World War I, though in Monte Carlo rather than Vienna. Puccini worked simultaneously on a "Grand Guignol" triptych of one-act operas: the horrific *Il tabarro* (*The Cloak*), the sentimental tragedy *Suor Angelica* and his one comedy, *Gianni Schicchi*, the most successful of the three. The triptych was premièred in New York in December 1918.

"Nessun dorma"

Puccini had lived since 1891 at his villa at Torre del Lago outside Lucca, with his wife Elvira (his married mistress until 1904). In 1909 their servant girl committed suicide when unjustly accused by the jealous Elvira of having an affair with Puccini. This tragedy may have inspired the character of Liù, the gentle, lovable slave girl in Puccini's last opera *Turandot*, based on an oriental fairy-tale. The work includes the aria "Nessun dorma", popularized by the "Three Tenors" at a concert staged in conjunction with the 1990

football World Cup in Italy. *Turandot* was destined to have a happy ending, when the cruel princess Turandot is outwitted by Prince Calaf and finally succumbs to love. But Puccini died of a heart attack during treatment for throat cancer in November 1924, leaving the final love duet unfinished.

ABOVE: A page from the manuscript score of La Bohème *(1896). Puccini has indicated Mimi's death with a skull and crossbones in the margin.*

Life and works

NATIONALITY: Italian

BORN: Lucca, 1858;
DIED: Brussels, 1924

SPECIALIST GENRES:
Italian opera.

MAJOR WORKS:
Manon Lescaut (1893);
La Bohème (1896);
Tosca (1900);
Madama Butterfly (1904);
Turandot (1926).

Richard Strauss

From time to time the cruellest discords are succeeded by exquisite suavities, that caress the ear with delight.

CAMILLE SAINT-SAËNS (1835–1921), OF "SALOME"

Richard Strauss, like Rachmaninov, was a composer who outlived his era. Elgar and Sibelius stopped composing shortly after World War I, perhaps realizing that the spirit of the age contradicted their personal artistic visions; but their contemporaries Strauss and Rachmaninov enjoyed a late Romantic Indian summer, oblivious to stylistic change.

Strauss was born in 1864, the son of the principal horn player in the Munich court orchestra. His father Franz played horn solos in the premières of Wagner's *Tristan und Isolde* (1865) and *Die Meistersinger von Nürnberg* (1868), but the young Richard first encountered Wagner's operas a few years later. A precociously gifted child, he had learnt the piano from the age of four and the violin from eight.

Strauss's first important work, the *Serenade* for wind instruments, was performed in Berlin in 1882 by

ABOVE: A portrait of the young Richard Strauss (1864–1949), probably dating from the 1890s.

members of the famous Meiningen Orchestra, whose conductor Hans von Bülow commissioned the young composer's Suite in B flat. During this period Strauss also wrote his First Horn Concerto, a cello sonata, a symphony (No. 2, premièred in New York), and several song settings. In the summer of 1885 Strauss became von Bülow's assistant at Meiningen, and took over from von Bülow a month later. From then on, his career was divided between conducting and composing.

Tone-poems

In 1886 Strauss moved on to the Munich court opera, where he became interested in the theories of Wagner and Arthur Schopenhauer, and in Liszt's tone-poems. His own first venture into this genre, *Aus Italien*, dates from 1886. Between 1889,

LEFT: Strauss directing an opera from the pit, 1929, by Wilhelm Viktor Krausz.

RIGHT: The frontispiece to the original piano score of Elektra *(1909), designed by Louis Corinth.*

when he moved to Weimar as assistant conductor to the court opera, and 1898, when he became chief conductor of the Royal Opera in Berlin, he wrote a sequence of seven magnificent tone-poems: *Don Juan*, *Macbeth*, *Tod und Verklärung* (*Death and Transfiguration*), *Till Eulenspiegels lustige Streiche* (*Till Eulenspiegel's Merry Pranks*), *Also sprach Zarathustra* (*Thus Spake Zarathustra*), *Don Quixote* and *Ein Heldenleben* (*A Hero's Life*). Together with the *Symphonia domestica* (1902–4) and *Ein Alpensinfonie* (1911–15), they represent Strauss's most important orchestral works.

Opera

However, it was in the field of opera that Strauss achieved fame. Inspired by his marriage in 1893 to the soprano Pauline de Ahna, he began his long love affair with the voice – especially the female voice. His first opera, *Guntram*

ABOVE: The Dresden Court Opera House, where many of Strauss's operas were performed.

(1894), was a failure, and his second, *Feuersnot* (*Fire Famine*, 1901), is rarely performed; but from *Salome* (1905) onwards he created a series of magnificent and individual works which are rarely out of the repertoire. *Salome* (based on Oscar Wilde's scandalous play) and *Elektra* (based on Sophocles' drama) caused international sensations owing to Strauss's explicit treatment of their subjects. Musically, both owe much to Wagner; *Salome* in particular is a masterpiece of sensuous, overblown late Romanticism. The royalties from *Salome* alone enabled Strauss to build himself a luxurious villa at Garmisch.

The librettist of *Elektra*, Hugo von Hofmannsthal (1874–1929), worked with Strauss over the next two decades: their most successful collaboration was the Mozartian comedy *Der Rosenkavalier*. With Hofmannsthal, Strauss went on to create *Ariadne auf Naxos*, *Die Frau ohne Schatten* (*The Woman without a Shadow*, 1914–17), *Die ägyptische Helena* (*The Egyptian Helen*, 1923–7) and *Arabella* (1929–32), completed after Hofmannsthal's death. Strauss's librettist for his next opera, *Die*

schweigsame Frau (*The Silent Woman*, 1933–4) was the Jewish Stefan Zweig, but the prevailing political climate in Germany required Strauss to choose an Austrian librettist, Joseph Gregor, for his subsequent operas: *Friedenstag* (*Peace Day*, 1935–6), *Daphne* (1936–7) and *Die Liebe der Danaë* (*Danaë's Love*, 1938–40).

Strauss's political naivety led to his exploitation by the Nazi Reichsmusik-kammer, which appointed him its president in 1933 but removed him two years later (his daughter-in-law was Jewish). He spent the war years in Vienna (where he wrote his last opera, *Capriccio,* in 1940–1), but afterwards moved to Switzerland while he was investigated – and eventually cleared of Nazi affiliations – by the denazification tribunal.

Strauss's last works are mainly instrumental: they include *Metamorphosen* for 23 solo strings (1945, a lament for the devastation of Germany), the Second Horn Concerto, the Oboe Concerto, sonatinas for wind instruments, and the radiant *Vier letzte Lieder* (*Four Last Songs*, 1948) for voice and orchestra. He died at his home in Garmisch, aged 85.

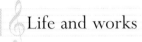

Life and works

NATIONALITY: German

BORN: Munich, 1864; **DIED:** Garmisch, 1949

SPECIALIST GENRES: Late Romantic tone-poems, Wagnerian-style opera.

MAJOR WORKS: Tone-poems *Macbeth* (1886–8), *Don Juan* (1888–9), *Tod und Verklärung* (1888–9), *Till Eulenspiegels lustige Streiche* (1894–5), *Also sprach Zarathustra* (1895–6), *Don Quixote* (1896–7) and *Ein Heldenleben* (1897–8); operas *Salome* (1905), *Elektra* (1909), *Der Rosenkavalier* (1911) and *Ariadne auf Naxos* (1911–12); *Capriccio* (1940–1); *Four Last Songs* (1948).

Sergei Rachmaninov

I feel like a ghost wandering in a world grown alien.
I cannot cast out the old way of writing and I cannot acquire the new.

RACHMANINOV

Rachmaninov was the last of a tradition of great pianist-composers, and the last of the Russian Romantics. The dramatic sweep of his music, combined with a haunting Russian melancholy, holds a powerful appeal. His three symphonies and four piano concertos are much loved.

He had his earliest piano lessons from his mother, a trained pianist. In 1882 his family moved to St Petersburg, where Rachmaninov entered the Conservatory. But when his parents separated, he transferred to Moscow, where he studied with the strict teacher Nikolay Zverev, and from 1888 onwards, with Alexander Ziloti (1863–1945) for piano and Anton Arensky (1861–1906) for composition. He graduated from the piano class of the Moscow Conservatory in the summer of 1891, completing his First Piano Concerto at the same time. The next year, his one-

ABOVE: Sergei Rachmaninov, painted in 1925 while he was living in the USA, by Konstantin Andreyevich Somov.

act opera *Aleko* won him the Conservatory's highest award for composition and, shortly after graduating, he wrote one of his most popular pieces, the Prelude in C sharp minor for piano.

In 1897, Rachmaninov's good luck changed when his First Symphony, in D minor, was performed at a Russian Symphony Concert, conducted by Alexander Glazunov. The performance was a disaster (Glazunov was rumoured to be drunk), and the critic César Cui described the piece as "a programme symphony on the Seven Plagues of Egypt". It was not

performed again until 1945. Rachmaninov suffered a nervous breakdown, and could not compose anything for three years. In due course he underwent a successful course of hypnotic treatment with a Dr Nikolay Dahl, which restored his confidence and enabled him to start work on the Second Piano Concerto, the theme of whose slow movement was used to memorable effect in David Lean's 1945 film *Brief Encounter*.

Rachmaninov gave the première of his new concerto, dedicated to Dr Dahl, on 9 November 1901, and a few months later, after finishing his cantata *Spring*, he married his cousin Natalya Satina. Over the next few years he occupied himself with opera composition, until the illness of his daughter Irina obliged the family to move to Dresden in 1906. There he completed his Second Symphony (the

ABOVE: Alexander Glazunov is reputed to have ruined the première of Rachmaninov's First Symphony by conducting while drunk.

ABOVE: Rachmaninov had unusually large hands, able to cope with big stretches — an advantage for a virtuoso pianist.

ABOVE: Red Square in Moscow, with St Basil's Cathedral illuminated. Rachmaninov drew inspiration from the Russian Orthodox liturgy, and wrote some fine sacred vocal music.

slow movement with its long-breathed clarinet solo is a masterly piece of writing), the First Piano Sonata, and the symphonic poem *The Isle of the Dead*, inspired by a painting by the Swiss artist Arnold Böcklin.

In 1909 Rachmaninov made his first visit to America, where he toured with a new work, the Third Piano Concerto. Over the next few years he spent the summers on his country estate, where he wrote the 13 Preludes for piano, Op. 13 (1910), the Liturgy of St John Chrysostom (1910), the *Etudes-tableaux* for piano, Op. 33 (1911), the 14 Songs, Op. 34, and the Second Piano Sonata (1913). During the winters he toured as a pianist, a routine that continued until the outbreak of World War I. His other major compositions of this period include the choral symphony *The Bells* (1913) and the *All-night Vigil* for unaccompanied choir (1915).

America

In 1917, the dangerous political situation in Russia forced Rachmaninov and his family into exile, first in Sweden, and then in America, where he remained for the rest of his life. From 1918 onwards he wrote little, spending most of his time performing. The Fourth Piano Concerto was written in 1926, but when it failed to achieve the success of its predecessors Rachmaninov was forced to revise and shorten it.

In 1931 he composed his last solo piano work, the *Variations on a Theme of Corelli*, followed by the brilliant *Rhapsody on a Theme of Paganini* for piano and orchestra (1934), the Third Symphony (1935–8), and the Symphonic Dances, his last work (1940). By early 1943 he was exhausted and ill, but he continued to tour. He died of cancer at his home in Beverly Hills on 28 March 1943, four days before his 70th birthday.

Life and works

NATIONALITY: Russian

BORN: Semyonovo, 1873; **DIED:** Beverly Hills, 1943

SPECIALIST GENRES: Piano concertos, solo piano music.

MAJOR WORKS: Four piano concertos; three symphonies; 24 Preludes for piano (1892–1910); *Rhapsody on a Theme of Paganini* (1934).

Glossary

Aria: an operatic solo.

Bel canto: (beautiful singing) Italian style of operatic singing, emphasizing beauty and evenness of tone and smooth phrasing.

Chromatic scale: a scale moving by semitones.

Clef: sign that indicates the pitch of notes written on the staff by fixing the position of one note.

Coda: extra section at the end of a movement.

Concerto: a work for solo instrument(s) and orchestra, usually in three movements.

Concerto grosso: instrumental form contrasting a small group of instruments with a larger orchestral group.

Counterpoint: the weaving together of two or more melodic lines to make musical sense, resulting in polyphony.

Development: in sonata form, the section of a movement following the initial statement of the themes, in which they are expanded or modified.

Exposition: the first part of sonata form, in which the main themes are stated.

Fugue: contrapuntal work in three or more parts of equal importance, which enter successively in imitation of each other.

Grand opera: 19th-century opera which is all sung, with no spoken dialogue.

Harmony: the simultaneous sounding of different notes.

Key: the classification of the notes of a scale, determined by the key-note.

Leitmotif: (leading motif) a short theme used repeatedly in a score – especially by Wagner – to denote an object, person or idea.

Libretto: the text of an opera or oratorio.

Madrigal: a contrapuntal setting in several parts of a secular verse.

Minuet: French rustic dance in triple time adapted to court use in the 17th century, and to symphonic use in the 18th century.

Motet: Ecclesiastical vocal musical form based on a given melody with other parts in counterpoint.

Motif, motive: a recognizable short group of notes in a work.

Motto theme: a theme that recurs during a piece of music, similar to a *Leitmotif*.

Nocturne: a short lyrical piece, usually for piano, in one movement.

Opera buffa: comic opera.

Opera seria: serious and formal Italian opera, with heroic or mythological plot.

Oratorio: an extended musical setting of a religious text in semi-dramatic form.

Ostinato: a persistently repeated musical phrase or rhythm.

Overture: (1) an orchestral opening movement to an opera, play or suite; (2) an orchestral work in one movement, usually with a title alluding to a literary or pictorial source.

Polyphony: the simultaneous sounding of different melodic lines, generally in counterpoint.

Prelude: a musical introduction, or a short self-contained piece.

Programme music: a piece of music interpreting a picture or story.

Recapitulation: in sonata form, the section which repeats the original themes after the development.

Recitative: speech-like singing in opera used for dialogue or to precede an aria.

Scherzo: (a joke) a lively movement in a symphony developed by Beethoven to take the place of the minuet and trio.

Sonata: an instrumental work in three or four movements and for one or two players.

Sonata form: a construction used in the first movement of a sonata or symphony, which is divided into three sections: exposition, development and recapitulation.

Song-cycle: a set of songs grouped by the composer in a particular order for performance, often based on a sequence of poems.

Staff (or stave): the five lines on which notes are written, the pitch being determined by the clef at the beginning.

Suite: an instrumental piece in several movements.

Symphony: a substantial orchestral work, usually in four movements: an allegro, a slow movement, a minuet or scherzo, then another allegro or rondo to finish.

Tonality: the general key of a piece.

Tone-poem: a substantial orchestral work intended to interpret a non-musical idea, picture or literary work.

Trio: (1) a combination of three performers; (2) a work for three performers; (3) the centre section of a minuet, traditionally written in three parts.

Index

Acknowledgements

The publisher would like to thank the following picture libraries for the use of their pictures in the book (l=left, r=right, t=top, b=bottom). Every effort has been made to acknowledge the pictures properly; however, we apologize if there are any unintentional omissions, which will be corrected in future editions.

AKG, London: 8–9; 15t; 16t; 27t; 30bl; 34bl; 44t, br; 47b; 48t; 64–5; 66t; 67t, br; 78b; 79t; 84b; 86b; *British Library* 10r; *Erich Lessing* 16b.
Art Archive Ltd: 15b; 50br; 59t; 85b.
Bridgeman Art Library, London: 1; 2; 3; 6l; 14; 17b; 18–19; 20–1; 22; 23b; 28t; 29; 30t; 33t, b; 34t; 35t; 36b; 38t; 39; 40b; 41t; 42–3; 44bl; 45t, b; 53b; 62t; 63b; 69b; 74br; 75l; 90t, bl, br; © *Arthur Rackham Estate* 79bl; *Novosti* 92t.

Camera Press: 53tl; 68br; 85t.
Eye Ubiquitous: *James Davis* 66b.
Getty: 70t; 91; 93.
Lebrecht Collection, London: 7tr, b; 10l; 11tr, b; 12; 13l, r; 17tl, tr; 23tl; 24t, b; 25t, bl, br; 26t, b; 28bl, br; 30br; 31t, b; 32t, bl, br; 34br; 35b; 36t; 37tl, tr, b; 38br; 40t; 41b; 46t, b; 47t; 48b; 49tl, tr, b; 50t, bl; 51t, b; 54t, bl, br; 55; 56; 57bl, br; 58t, bl, br; 59b; 60t; 61t, b; 62bl; 63tl, tr; 67bl; 68t, bl; 69t; 70bl, br; 71t, b; 72t, bl; 73b; 74t; 76t, bl, br; 77l, r; 78t; 80t, bl, br; 81t, b; 82t; 84t; 86t; 87t, b; 88t, bl, br; 89t, b; 92bl, br; 94; *M. Allen* 38bl; *Arthur Reynolds Collection* 82b; 83t, b; *Matti Kolho* 75r; *S. Lauterwasser* 79br; *Peter Mares* 53tr; *B. Morris* 23tr; 52b; 57t; 62br; *Celene Rosen* 11tl; *Royal Academy of Music* 60b; 74bl; *G. Salter* 72br.
Performing Arts Library: *Clive Barda* 27b; *Fritz Curzon* 52t.
Wendy Thompson: *Harold T. Storey* 73t.